Praise for

Still Broke

"Rick Wartzman proves, once again, why he is America's most compelling historian of corporate culture. *Still Broke* is fair-minded, exacting, and brutally clear that achieving humane wages for frontline workers will take more than good intentions. This should be required reading for every CEO, union leader, and politician in America."

—Evan Osnos, staff writer, *New Yorker*, and author of *Wildland*

"*Still Broke* is an important, comprehensive, supremely balanced study of how Walmart treats its workers. Despite a close and cooperative relationship with Walmart, Wartzman pulls no punches in his efforts to pass judgment on his corporate subject's incomplete efforts to do right by its employees. It's totally absorbing."

—Adam Lashinsky, author of *Wild Ride*

"With nuance and unparalleled access, Wartzman thoughtfully dissects the 'corporate Rashomon' that is Walmart. *Still Broke* is a fast-paced narrative that offers essential and sobering insights at a pivotal moment for industrial relations."

—Miriam Pawel, author of *The Crusades of Cesar Chavez* and *The Union of Their Dreams*

"*Still Broke* is a 360-degree portrait of Walmart, a company that has for years been a synonym for 'greed.' Wartzman's reporting on the corporation and its history is balanced and thorough. He concludes with well-reasoned solutions that might improve this case study in extreme capitalism, including raising the minimum wage higher than you might expect. The book is that rare title that is for corporate consultants *and* community organizers."

—Alissa Quart, executive director, the Economic Hardship Reporting Project, and author of *Squeezed*

"*Still Broke* is a look behind the curtain at the inner workings of one of the world's most controversial corporations. With thorough and excellent reporting and research, Wartzman delivers a portrait of Walmart that contains a number of surprises. Still, anyone who reads through to the book's stunning final chapter will know that Wartzman doesn't hold back. He understands exactly what's ailing this country."

—Michael Tomasky, editor, the *New Republic*, and author of *The Middle Out*

"Walmart, in Wartzman's fascinating account, is not the caricature of evildoing popular on the left side of Twitter. Yet *Still Broke* returns us to the most fundamental question about America's value proposition, built around the value of a good hour's work. If even corporations like Walmart, which seems to have bought into its broader responsibilities toward society, cannot find it in their interest to provide a decent living to the workers who toil for them, should they be left to set the rules?"

—Eduardo Porter, columnist, Bloomberg Opinion, and former Economic Scene columnist, the *New York Times*

Still Broke

Also by Rick Wartzman

The End of Loyalty: The Rise and Fall of Good Jobs in America

What Would Drucker Do Now?: Solutions to Today's Toughest Challenges from the Father of Modern Management

Obscene in the Extreme: The Burning and Banning of John Steinbeck's The Grapes of Wrath

The King of California: J.G. Boswell and the Making of a Secret American Empire
(coauthored with Mark Arax)

Still Broke

Walmart's Remarkable Transformation and the Limits of Socially Conscious Capitalism

Rick Wartzman

PUBLICAFFAIRS
New York

PublicAffairs
Hachette Book Group
1290 Avenue of the Americas, New York, NY 10104
www.publicaffairsbooks.com
@Public_Affairs

Printed in the United States of America

First Edition: November 2022

Published by PublicAffairs, an imprint of Perseus Books, LLC, a subsidiary of Hachette Book Group, Inc. The PublicAffairs name and logo is a trademark of the Hachette Book Group.

Print book interior design by Six Red Marbles.

Library of Congress Cataloging-in-Publication Data

Names: Wartzman, Rick, author.
Title: Still broke : Walmart's remarkable transformation and the limits of socially conscious capitalism / Rick Wartzman.
Description: First edition. | New York : PublicAffairs, 2022. | Includes bibliographical references and index.
Identifiers: LCCN 2022013116 | ISBN 9781541757998 (hardcover) | ISBN 9781541757981 (ebook)
Subjects: LCSH: Wal-Mart (Firm)—Finance. | Wal-Mart (Firm)—Employees—Finance, Personal. | Wal-Mart (Firm)—Management. | Social responsibility of business—United States. | United States—Economic conditions—21st century.
Classification: LCC HF5429.215.U6 W37 2022 | DDC 381/.14906573—dc23/eng/20220323
LC record available at https://lccn.loc.gov/2022013116

ISBNs: 9781541757998 (hardcover), 9781541757981 (ebook)

LSC-C

Printing 1, 2022

For Emma and Nathaniel, who have made me incredibly proud as I've watched you take your own blank pages and create upon them

For Randye, forever

CONTENTS

AUTHOR'S NOTE

IN 2017, Wal-Mart Stores Inc. changed its name to Walmart Inc. I use "Walmart" throughout the text for continuity, even in references preceding the switchover. The endnotes use both spellings.

CHAPTER 1

Mr. Sam's Bargain

IN LATE MARCH 2020, with the coronavirus spreading so fast that President Donald Trump had been forced to back off his expressed hope of packing people into churches on Easter, I tuned in to a Monday morning webinar to check out how several major corporations were responding to the pandemic. It was so early in the crisis that the nation's COVID-19 death count hadn't even hit 10,000, and the Centers for Disease Control and Prevention had yet to recommend that masks be worn in public. Zoom still seemed more like a blessing than a burden. But things were grim and clearly getting grimmer.

The session had been put together by FSG, a consulting firm, and featured executives from Truist Financial, 3M, and Walmart discussing how they were "changing policies to better support their most vulnerable workers." "Every day I find myself using the word 'unprecedented,'" Greg Hills, the co-CEO of FSG, said as he started off the discussion. With "businesses shuttered, schools and colleges emptied, and social life all but suspended," as that day's *New York Times* put it, this was "the scariest time that I've lived in," Hills added.

"I'm scared for my mother," he went on. "I'm scared for my wife and kids, for my friends, my extended family. I'm not sleeping well at night because I'm worried about and feel responsible for the livelihoods of 150 employees at FSG."

Julie Gehrki, a vice president at Walmart's philanthropic foundation, nodded empathetically on the screen, though it must have been hard not to consider that, as taxing as it was to tend to 150 people, it was up to her company to look after 10,000 times that many workers across all 50 states. Headquartered in Bentonville, Arkansas, the nation's biggest employer boasted 1.5 million people on its US payroll—roughly equal to the population of Philadelphia, or twice that of Seattle—plus 700,000 more in two dozen other countries. By comparison, Amazon has about 1.1 million US employees; Target, 350,000; Costco, 190,000.

When it was Gehrki's turn to speak, she highlighted steps that Walmart had taken to care for this multitude, particularly its one million domestic frontline workers—or "associates," as the company prefers to call them. Walmart's senior team, she said, had recently huddled through a weekend to devise an emergency leave policy so that if employees didn't feel well or were uncomfortable being inside a store, they could miss work and wouldn't be punished. The company was offering them free telemedicine. It had trimmed its shopping hours so crews could deep-clean Walmart's more than 5,000 US locations every night, and it was busy putting up plastic "sneeze guards" to protect its cashiers and pharmacists. It was placing decals on store floors to make it easier for customers to keep six feet apart.

A week before, Walmart had said it would hand out $550 million in bonuses to its hourly workers, the first of several such payments that would eventually total more than $2.5 billion. To satisfy Americans' endless appetite for household goods and groceries while they hunkered down at home and stockpiled essentials, as well as to backfill for those workers who were now going out on leave, the company had also turbocharged its hiring process. In the span of just a month, it would bring aboard 150,000 new employees and then announce that it was hiring 50,000 more—many of them as part of a coordinated, multi-industry effort to absorb restaurant and hospitality workers who'd been let go from their jobs. "We are really leaning into everything we can do," Gehrki said.

As the event wrapped up, I downed the last of my coffee and began to sift through my inbox to see what messages I'd missed over the previous hour. One jumped out. Twenty minutes into the webinar—just as Gehrki was about to make her opening remarks—an email had landed from Andrea Dehlendorf, the co-executive director of United for Respect, a labor advocacy group that had grown out of the United Food and Commercial Workers union. "We have always been committed to ensuring that the voices of people working low-wage jobs are heard," Dehlendorf said in her missive, which trumpeted the 39 news stories her organization had helped to plant over the previous week. Many of them focused on Walmart, and their depiction was nothing like the one Gehrki had just presented.

The most biting critique came from Melissa Love, who stocked shelves part-time at a Walmart in Long Beach, California. In a

New York Times op-ed, the 27-year-old conveyed the tremendous stress she was under as customers snatched up practically every item they could. "It's been a lot like Black Friday," Love wrote, referring to the frenzied day after Thanksgiving that marks the kickoff of the holiday buying season. "I'm young and healthy, but I'm worried I will catch the coronavirus and infect my father."

After four years at Walmart, Love was earning $13.27 an hour, which penciled out to a little more than $20,000 per year for the 30 hours or so she worked each week while juggling her studies at Los Angeles Trade Technical College. Her pandemic bonus, which Gehrki had touted, would amount to all of 150 bucks. (Full-timers would receive $300.) At the moment, Love was the sole breadwinner in her household. Her dad, a shuttle-bus driver at Disneyland, had just been laid off—one of the millions of Americans whose jobs vaporized as the virus ravaged the economy.

In her piece in the *Times*, Love took issue with Walmart's new leave policy. She explained that the company was "allowing workers who test positive for the coronavirus to stay home for up to two weeks, but it will cut pay in half for any needed sick time after that." She said she feared that she or one of her coworkers might well wind up facing "the impossible choice of going to work sick and possibly infecting others or risking our already precarious finances." An active member of United for Respect, Love didn't hold back: "We make corporations like Walmart profitable—it's time for them to ensure we have enough to live on."

My head swirled. Where in this muddle did reality lie? Was Walmart as responsive to the needs of its employees as it was making itself out to be? Or was it as indifferent as Love claimed, bent on fattening its bottom line, the well-being of its workers be damned? For more than a year, prior to the outbreak of COVID-19, I'd been wrestling with these questions. However, answering them wasn't so easy, at least not anymore.

There was a time, for about a decade and a half beginning around the year 2000, when portraying Walmart as greedy, if not downright malevolent, had become as commonplace for many people as grabbing a quart of milk from the store. "If you really—we mean *really*—want to scare the locals next Halloween, here's an early costume idea for you or your kids: dress up as Walmart," two commentators wrote in 2008. Tellingly, this zinger didn't come from a pair of union backers or liberal pols or chin-scratchers from some left-wing think tank. It was served up by two officials from the normally staid corridors of the Federal Reserve Bank.

"Walmart has been fingered as the source of virtually every conceivable economic ill," they declared. "It kills jobs and downtowns, say critics, and destroys community character. It's been accused of discriminating against women, using illegal immigrants, requiring work off the clock, and being overly aggressive in stopping the formation of labor unions among its workers. It's been blamed for sprawl and traffic congestion, as well as aesthetic offenses."

A distinct genre of literature emerged during this period panning the company's avaricious behavior: *The Case Against Walmart*, *Slam-Dunking Walmart*, *The Bully of Bentonville*, *How Walmart Is Destroying America (and the World)*. An off-Broadway musical, *Walmartopia*, took aim at what its creator called "the cost of unfettered capitalism." Whereas General

Motors was widely perceived as having used its perch atop the list of America's biggest companies to help build the middle class after World War II, with union agreements that bestowed good pay and generous benefits and job security for generations of blue-collar workers, Walmart, now the largest corporation of them all, had come to symbolize something very different: a race-to-the-bottom brand of capitalism that was leaving legions of people struggling to get by. "Low prices are great," *BusinessWeek* asserted in a 2003 article. "But Walmart's dominance creates problems—for suppliers, workers, communities, and even American culture."

In fairness, much of the condemnation leveled at the company was too broad-brush. Plenty of cities and towns in America welcomed Walmart, eager for residents to be able to purchase quality goods at very low prices. "I tell people all the time: I was a big-time Walmart shopper when I was buying diapers, a big-time Walmart shopper when I was buying school supplies," said Marc Morial, the president of the National Urban League, who served as mayor of New Orleans from 1994 to 2002. "It's inexpensive, and the selection is wide." Others were delighted for a different reason to have a Walmart (or two, or three, or more) around: it brought jobs. "I'd rather have a person on somebody's payroll—even if it isn't at the highest wage—than on the unemployment roll," said John Mack, a civic leader in Los Angeles, as he reflected on Walmart's plans to make a giant foray into the region in 2003. More than 75 percent of the store managers at Walmart came up through the hourly ranks. The company was willing to hire those who'd been incarcerated, and it guaranteed a job offer to any honorably discharged US military veteran within his or her first year off active duty.

For a good many people, a job at Walmart "saved them from situations that were far worse," whether that meant "going hungry, getting evicted, having one's electricity turned off," or suffering some other blow, as two Columbia University sociologists, Adam Reich and Peter Bearman, found when they engaged in an extensive study of the company and United for Respect's campaign to upgrade conditions there. "Associates are not choosing between unionized jobs at GM and Walmart," they pointed out. "Assuming that there are jobs to choose from, Walmart workers are choosing between Walmart and McDonald's" or some other employer furnishing scanty wages. "They are comparing work to loneliness, isolation, sitting on a porch watching absolutely nothing ever happen, or playing video games." For lots of people, Walmart was their best chance to feel useful, to enjoy some camaraderie, to carve out an identity, to make something better of themselves. Reich and Bearman took note that when Walmart opened two stores in Washington, DC, in 2013, 23,000 people applied for 600 slots. Just how awful, then, could the company be?

Yet despite the positives, Walmart was long the object of widespread derision because this much was inescapable: it stinted on its workers to a degree that was difficult for many to stomach. Although a Walmart job might have been more appealing to many than the available alternatives, tens of thousands of the company's employees still couldn't make ends meet without their paychecks being leavened by government food stamps, Medicaid, or the succor of a nonprofit. "In orientation, we learned that the store's success depends entirely on us, the associates; in fact, our bright blue vests bear the statement 'At Walmart our people make the difference,'" Barbara Ehrenreich wrote in *Nickel and Dimed*, her renowned 2001 account of working a string of low-paying jobs, including in the apparel department of a Minneapolis Walmart for $7 an hour—a wage so measly she couldn't afford housing. "Underneath those vests, though, there are real-life charity cases, maybe even shelter dwellers," Ehrenreich added. Jon Lehman, who managed several Walmarts in Kentucky, used to keep a Rolodex on his desk with the phone numbers of nearby social service agencies at the ready. "I would call in the event that an associate came into my office and said, 'I can't afford to take my child to the doctor,' 'I can't afford groceries,' or 'I'm getting kicked out of my house,'" he said. "Many times, I would take the worker down to the United Way in my truck. They didn't know what to do."

In 2005, those championing a "living wage" throughout America issued a report that zeroed in on why so many industries—retail, janitorial, homecare, childcare, security, and hospitality—paid so little. They cited the failure of Congress to increase the minimum wage so that it kept up with inflation, the rising use of contractors and temp workers, the effects of globalization, and the decline of unions. And, finally, they singled out one other culprit: "the Walmart-ization of the economy." It was a phenomenon defined as "the proliferation of the Walmart business model and its central tenet: the merciless squeezing of labor costs to eliminate retail competition."

As the years rolled on, Walmart did little to shake this reputation, even as it burnished its image—through both word and deed—in other areas, most notably by becoming more environmentally conscious. In November 2013, the company caused a stir when its store in Canton, Ohio, set out a bunch of purple and orange storage bins for workers to share food with one another so that, as the sign read, "Associates in Need can enjoy Thanksgiving dinner." An employee, who said she found the gesture "demoralizing" and "kind of depressing," snapped photographs of the bins and sent them to United for Respect, which passed them right along to the media. The reaction was swift. "That captures Walmart right there," said Kate Bronfenbrenner, who taught at Cornell University's School of Industrial and Labor Relations. "Its employees don't make enough to feed themselves and their families." Ashton Kutcher, the actor, tweeted at the company: "Is your profit margin so important you can't pay your employees enough to be above the poverty line?"

Walmart characterized the episode in Canton as "part of the company's culture to rally around associates and take care of them" and said it was "unfortunate that an act of human kindness has been taken so out of context." Few bought it. The *Cleveland Plain Dealer* fielded a poll in which they asked people what they thought about the incident. Of the 20,000 respondents, 88 percent said it illustrated that "Walmart needs to pay its employees better wages." Only 8 percent said the program "helps Walmart employees through their hardships." As evenhanded as they were in their analysis, Reich and Bearman couldn't help but draw the same conclusion: such a food drive "wouldn't be necessary," they wrote, "if Walmart didn't put people in such desperate straits to begin with."

But then the picture got more complicated. In 2015, Walmart upped its lowest hourly wage from the federal minimum of $7.25 to $10 in two stages. It also revamped the system that set employee work schedules, hoping to give more predictability to some and more flexibility to others, depending on their needs.

In addition, Walmart got serious about skills training as it sought to forge new routes for someone to go from an entry-level job to a middle-class career in retail or another field. Taken together, this bundle of improvements "got our associates to a place where they recognized we were listening to them and that we were going to invest in them and that we cared about them and we wanted to retain them," said Doug McMillon, who became Walmart's chief executive in 2014.

Even United for Respect had to concede that something extraordinary was taking place. "If you look at Walmart, over its 50-year existence, they've always prided themselves on saying our employees are going to be the lowest-paid," observed Dan Schlademan, a cofounder with Dehlendorf of United for Respect and its co-executive director. "Now they've changed their business model." Barry Ritholtz, a maverick wealth manager who in the past had branded Walmart a "corporate welfare queen" because so many of its employees were on public assistance, agreed. "These are not minor adjustments," he said. "The company seems to have found some religion" in terms of "how it treats its workers."

Walmart followed its 2015 pay increase with another in 2018, elevating its starting wage to $11 an hour. "A decade ago, the notion that Walmart could help corporate America find its soul would have been laughable," *Boston Globe* columnist Shirley Leung wrote. "Today, Walmart and McMillon are no joke when it comes to showing how companies can do well and do good."

In 2020, Walmart began to marshal workers into small teams and cross-train them to perform a range of assignments: displaying merchandise, pricing it correctly, upholding standards, and troubleshooting for customers. The arrangement resulted in an immediate pay raise for about 15 percent of the company's hourly workforce—with wages for some roles climbing from $11 to $15 an hour—and the promise that many more employees would soon have enhanced opportunities, as well. "With teaming, we gave them complete autonomy to help fix the things that they saw in their area," said Tyler Bursey, the manager of a Walmart in North Richland Hills, Texas, who himself started at the company as a cart pusher. "One of the biggest selling points I could give to them was, 'We want you to take ownership of whatever you see that needs to be done throughout the day.'"

As part of the reorganization, Walmart also ushered in a new position: "team lead," whose pay would start at $18 an hour and could get up to $30 in one of its 3,500 Supercenters—the biggest of big-boxes, selling everything from fishing rods to fresh trout, from apple juice to Apple iPhones. One hundred and five thousand of these team leads would supplant 145,000 department managers, whose hourly pay started at $12 and topped out at about $25. The new job would be less about tackling tasks and more about setting goals, delegating, and developing others to be effective. "It's unlocking the potential of our frontline associates," said Drew Holler, a senior vice president charged with overseeing the design and implementation of the new team structure. Amid all the shuffling, Walmart's overall employee headcount would stay steady as it doubled the number of "personal shoppers" to accommodate its burgeoning pickup and delivery business.

In 2021, Walmart boosted pay again—twice. The first move took 425,000 of its workers, including personal shoppers, to between $13 and $19 an hour. The second increased hourly wages for 565,000 employees by at least a dollar. The company also raised its minimum wage to $12 (and to as much as $17 in some stores). Its average hourly wage was now $16.40. It also said that it was establishing more full-time jobs and relying less on part-time labor to augment its workers' earnings and give them additional stability. Walmart has "gone from being seen as a problem to becoming a significant part of the solution," said John Streur, the chief executive of Calvert Research and Management, which specializes in socially responsible investing.

Alan Murray, the president of *Fortune* magazine and an exponent of the viewpoint that business is poised to lead the way in solving some of society's most intractable challenges, had likewise determined that the company was undergoing a historic shift. "Walmart founder Sam Walton famously paid the lowest price the market would bear for *everything*—labor included," he wrote. "Current CEO Douglas McMillon has taken a different approach."

Different in this regard, yes, but it wasn't as if the company had been trying to distance itself from Walton. His maxims plastered the walls of the Home Office in Bentonville and the breakrooms of stores. His autobiography, *Sam Walton: Made in America*, was required reading for anybody who hoped to get somewhere at the company. Every time I had a chance to talk to McMillon, he'd impart a pearl or two of wisdom from "Mr. Sam," as he is affectionately known. Other Walmart executives would invariably do the same. Although Walton died in 1992, his spirit is alive and well.

The funny thing was, those from United for Respect were also quick to summon Walton's management doctrine, thrilled with trying to turn his wisdom back on the company. Among "Sam's Rules for Building a Business" that they liked to invoke was this: "Share your profits with all your associates, and treat them as partners."

Whatever argument you were trying to make about working for Walmart—whether you believed the company was emblematic of a new age of enlightened capitalism or that it was still falling short of its founder's ideals—Mr. Sam was bound to be your touchstone. That's because there were shards of truth in all of it.

By the time Sam Walton opened the first Walmart in Rogers, Arkansas (about eight miles down the road from his adopted home of Bentonville), in 1962, not only did he have a clear-eyed vision of what he was trying to do, he knew how he was going to get there. With 22 years in the retail business at that point, Walton was a tiger, not a tyro.

Gutsy, magnetic, hypercompetitive, and shrewd as hell, he had soaked in one lesson after another about how to give American consumers exactly what they wanted. Born in Kingfisher, Oklahoma, Walton was raised mostly in small-town Missouri. His dad did all sorts of things: farming, banking, insurance, real estate. "We never thought of ourselves as poor," Walton said, "although we certainly didn't have much of what you'd call disposable income lying around." In 1940, straight out of college, Walton joined J. C. Penney as a management trainee, and although he left after about 18 months, the experience made a lasting impression.

"It was at Penney that Walton first came across many of the management ideas that, decades later, would popularly be thought of as his own," the journalist Bob Ortega has noted.

"One such idea was calling workers 'associates,' as a way of making them feel more like partners in the business.... Another was 'management by walking around,' as some would label Walton's habit of incessantly visiting his own stores. These visits let him see firsthand how local managers were doing, pass on tips to them about how to do this or that better, pick up on anything new they might have come up with, and, of course, meet all the workers."

In 1945, after two years in the Army, Walton snapped up a Ben Franklin store in Newport, Arkansas, for $25,000—$5,000 of which he and his wife, Helen, had saved and the rest borrowed from his father-in-law. He was 27 and full of ambition. Newport, nestled along the White River in the northeast part of the state, surrounded by pecan and cotton farms, only had about 5,000 people. But Walton's aim was to make his Ben Franklin the most profitable variety store in all of Arkansas within five years.

Ben Franklin tightly prescribed the ways in which its franchisees were to run things, and Walton was gung-ho for such guidance. "They had their own accounting system, with manuals telling you what to do, when, and how," Walton would recollect. "They had merchandise statements, they had accounts-payable sheets, they had little ledger books called Beat Yesterday books, in which you could compare this year's sales with last year's on a day-by-day basis." For Walton—full of gumption but still green—it was almost like going to grad school.

What the company couldn't teach him, he learned from his competitors, including a Sterling Store across the street that was pulling in double the sales of Walton's Ben Franklin when he first got to Newport. He scrutinized his rival's pricing and displays and other tricks of the trade—and imitated what worked best, a maneuver he'd carry with him to Walmart. He exhibited a keenness for experimentation and a flair for promotion, as well, wooing customers with a popcorn maker and an ice cream machine out on the sidewalk.

When the Ben Franklin bureaucracy bridled Walton, he made an end run around it, disregarding the parent company's preferred supplier network and finding cheaper manufacturers and wholesalers to cut deals with him. By doing so, he said, "it got me thinking in the direction of what eventually became the foundation of Walmart's philosophy": If you can hold down your costs, you can pass along those savings to your customers in the form of lower prices. And if that brings enough customers through the door, the volume will translate into even more profit than if the markups had been higher. "That is where it started," said Bud Walton, Sam's younger brother, who became his sibling's assistant manager in Newport. "Our money was made by controlling expenses."

By 1950, Walton had met his original objective and then some. His Ben Franklin was the largest variety store in Arkansas and the chain's leader in sales and profits across a six-state region. But there would be no celebration. Walton had botched his lease on the building, neglecting to include an option to renew. His landlord, who wanted to give his son a leg up in retailing, took the property back. "It was the low point of my business life," Walton would later say. "I felt sick to my stomach." Angry and embarrassed, Walton became "a little more wary of just how tough the world can be," but there was nothing to be done: "I had to pick myself up and get on with it, do it all over again, only even better this time."

Sam and Helen moved to Bentonville and bought an old variety store on the town square. They also acquired the barbershop next door so they could demolish the dividing wall and double their space. Bentonville was even tinier than Newport, but relocating to northwest Arkansas had its virtues. It put Helen closer to her family in Oklahoma and gave Sam the perfect spot for quail hunting, which was dear to his own heart. The new store bore the name Walton's Five and Dime, and from the get-go Sam proved to have what every merchant fancies: a nose for what his customers would find irresistible.

"He was always thinking up new things to try in the store," recalled Inez Threet, who worked at Walton's Five and Dime. "One time he made a trip to New York, and he came back a few days later and said, 'Come here, I want to show you something. This is going to be the item of the year.' I went over and looked at a bin full of—I think they called them zori sandals—they call them thongs now. And I just laughed and said, 'No way will those things sell. They'll just blister your toes.' Well, he took them and tied them together in pairs and dumped them all on a table at the end of an aisle for 19 cents a pair. And they just sold like you wouldn't believe. I have never seen an item sell as fast, one after another, just piles of them. Everybody in town had a pair."

But Walton was too much of a go-getter to stay put in Bentonville, and within a few years he opened additional Ben Franklin stores in towns all over Arkansas, southern Missouri, and Kansas. He also embraced a new format—a testament to Walton's knack for innovation. In Fayetteville, Arkansas, he became one of the first retailers in the country to have cash registers up front rather than counters spread all around the store (similar to a makeup counter at a Nordstrom or Saks Fifth

Avenue today). Instead of waiting for one clerk after another to retrieve the things they wanted, shoppers could now move more easily throughout the whole store with "lightweight shopping baskets in which to gather your choices as you go," as Walton expounded in an ad heralding the then-unfamiliar "self-service" layout. With the new setup, Walton could also get away with fewer workers and less specialized training, keeping his labor costs down.

By 1962, Walton was the biggest variety-store owner and biggest Ben Franklin franchisee in the country, with 16 outlets he'd bounce between via his own private plane, a single-engine Tri-Pacer. Yet even with all he'd accomplished, he had been getting nervous for a couple of years now. A new crop of competitors—discount stores—had sprung up around the country, and they were growing so fast that Walton couldn't ignore the threat. E.J. Korvette, Spartan's, Zayre, Mammoth Mart, and others had discovered a winning formula: no-frills stores in low-rent districts that offered consumers a huge inventory at bargain prices. Gibson Products of Dallas, not far from Walton's own backyard, lived by the motto "Buy it low, stack it high, sell it cheap."

"I knew the discount idea was the future," Walton said, and it played right into the instincts he had started to hone back in Newport: you could make a ton of money by selling a mountain of stuff that didn't cost a whole lot. Walton took a couple of stabs at finding a partner for his new venture, but he got nowhere. It was time to strike out on his own.

That first Walmart in Rogers—"Wal-Mart Discount City"—was, at its core, not very different from the thousands of Walmarts that would follow. In ads for the July 2 grand opening, the store pledged to provide "everyday low prices." This was much more than a slogan; it was an ethos. "From day one of Walmart, Mr. Walton made it clear that this wasn't just Ben Franklin with low prices on some items," remembered Charlie Cate, a manager. "He wanted real discounting. He said, 'We want to discount everything we carry.' When the other chains around us weren't discounting, he said, 'We advertise that we sell for less, and we mean it!' So whatever else we did, we always had to sell for less. If an item came in and everybody else in town was selling it for 25 cents, we'd go with 21 cents." With many retailers charging the manufacturer's suggested price, the savings you could get at Walmart were something to behold: $11.88 versus $17.95 for a Sunbeam iron; $74.37 versus $100 for a Polaroid camera; $5.97 versus $10.80 for a Wilson baseball mitt.

The very same year that Walton got into the discount business, the bug bit others. Harry Cunningham, president of the Kresge five-and-dime chain, opened his first discount store, Kmart, in a suburb of Detroit in March 1962 with plans to open 37 more. Three months later, the variety-store operator Woolworth opened its first Woolco discount store in Ohio. The Minneapolis-based regional department store chain Dayton Corporation also opened four discount houses, named Target, in 1962.

But Walton avoided the crush of competition. While most discounters set their sights on larger metropolitan areas, Walton expanded only into towns with fewer than 25,000 people, and oftentimes far fewer. Others thought he was crazy, that there was no way these hamlets could ever sustain the enterprise. But Walton deduced that if locals could find the same goods at the same low prices at Walmart that they'd otherwise have to drive an hour or more to get, they'd be glad to give him their business. And he'd have the market pretty much to himself.

As the 1960s wound to a close, Walton owned 18 Walmarts in three states: two in Oklahoma, five in Missouri, and 11 in Arkansas. One was in Newport, where Walton ran his old landlord's son out of business. Although Walton would insist that this wasn't an act of revenge—merely the natural consequence of winning over the other guy's customers—his store manager in Newport said the boss left little doubt about what he wanted done to the landlord's boy. "Break him!" Walton said. And he did. (Walton's edge would also reveal itself on the tennis court, where, in the words of one of his first managers, "he could be playing a one-legged man in a wheelchair, and he would show no mercy.")

To be sure, these first Walmarts weren't terribly advanced. "We didn't have ordering programs. We didn't have a basic merchandise assortment. We certainly didn't have any sort of computers," Walton would say years later. "But we managed to sell our merchandise as low as we possibly could, and that kept us right-side-up for the first 10 years—that and consistently improving our sales in these smaller markets by building up our relationship with the customers. The idea was simple: when customers thought of Walmart, they should think of low prices and satisfaction guaranteed."

Over time, Walmart got more sophisticated. Some of this was due to Walton's tried-and-true method of dissecting what other retailers were up to—and then knocking off whatever was most advantageous. Don Soderquist, who would become a top Walmart executive, never forgot going into a Kmart near his house on a Saturday and happening upon Walton, who was in sponge mode. At the time, Soderquist was in charge of data processing at Ben Franklin's main offices in Chicago, and he had just been in a meeting with Walton the day before. "I thought, 'What the heck is he doing way out here?'" Soderquist recounted.

"I strolled up behind him, and I could hear him asking this clerk, 'Well, how frequently do you order?...Uh-huh....How much do you order?...And if you order on a Tuesday, when does the merchandise come in?' He's writing everything she says down in a little blue spiral notebook. Then Sam gets down on his hands and knees and he's looking under this stack table, and he opens the sliding doors and says, 'How do you know how much you've got under here when you're placing that order?' Finally, I said, 'Sam Walton, is that you?' And he looked up from the floor and said, 'Oh, Don! Hi! What are you doing here?' I said, 'I'm shopping. What are you doing?' And he said, 'Oh, this is just part of the educational process. That's all.'"

In the late 1960s, Walton began to invest—albeit in many cases reluctantly, given his parsimonious disposition—in warehousing and information technology. In 1970, he'd take Walmart public, fueling a surge of expansion that vaulted the company from a fairly obscure regional retailer into one of the nation's four biggest discounters, though its business would remain concentrated for the time being in the South and Midwest. Historian Nelson Lichtenstein, who has chronicled Walmart's ascent as closely as anyone, has termed the 1970s the company's "miracle decade," in part because its prosperity stood in such contrast to that of other retail chains, which foundered under the era's double-whammy of high prices and high unemployment. Walmart's pace of growth was four to five times that of J. C. Penney, Kmart, and Woolco. "For most discounters,"

Lichtenstein has written, "the combination of inflation and recession—stagflation it was called—made for an economic environment that was poison. Clustered in cities and suburbs, they were locked into a fierce, profit-draining price competition, even as wages, interest payments, and shipping costs soared. But Walmart, with most of its stores in small towns and exurbs, escaped this trap. Many of Walmart's rural customers... actually benefited from the burst of 1970s inflation as land and farm commodity prices rose rapidly."

Through the decade, Walmart opened as many as 50 new stores per year; revenue rose at an annual clip of nearly 40 percent. And it was bringing on an average of almost 100 new workers every week, so that by the end of the '70s, the company employed 21,000 people. Even at this scale, however, many of those working for Walmart felt a special attachment to the business, a bond that rested largely on two things: cash and charisma.

The cash came through a profit-sharing plan that Walton—with an assist from Helen—put in place in 1971 for all workers who had been with the company for at least two years. It was an extension of a perk that had originally gone only to salaried managers. (In 1976, the requirement was reduced to one year, while it took seven years to become fully vested.) Once an employee retired, they were eligible to take out their share, which had been invested in the interim, mostly in Walmart stock.

For many it was a godsend, especially considering how little they had made otherwise, even after the company tacked on nominal bonuses for stimulating higher sales or curbing "shrinkage" (losses from employee theft, shoplifting, damage, cashier error, and so on). Walton had always done all he could to tamp down his workers' regular pay, going so far as to configure the company in its early days in a manner that would circumvent the federal minimum wage. Even after a US District Court judge thwarted that penny-pinching gambit, Walton copped to still being "chintzy" with his hourly workers. Retailers paid poorly by and large, and Walmart was no exception. But the company's profit sharing, supplemented by another sweetener that enabled employees to buy Walmart stock for relatively little, gave Walton a mechanism to engender their loyalty—and stave off early attempts by the Retail Clerks Union to organize them.

"Building a 'nest egg' for us is a definite plus in our lives," said Bette Hendrix, the corporate assistant secretary, "and is an incentive to do our utmost in job performance to increase that 'nest egg' by our own actions and attitudes." Michael Bergdahl witnessed the effect during his time as a Walmart human resources executive in Bentonville. "Because of profit sharing... the associates worried about saving the company money as much as the company leaders did," he said. "I saw it happening every day in my own department. The associates brought the basic office necessities from their homes to outfit their desks, including pens, pencils, staplers, staples, paper clips, Post-It notes, rubber bands, highlighter pens, tape, and calculators. I can assure you that no one in management told them to do this; it was something the associates themselves reinforced culturally." Their impetus was straightforward: they wanted to save Walmart money "in order to directly impact their own profit sharing," according to Bergdahl, "and it happened all around the company." No wonder Walton called profit sharing "the move we made that I'm proudest of." It has, he said, "pretty much been the carrot that's kept Walmart headed forward."

While high rates of employee turnover—endemic throughout retail—limited the breadth of profit sharing, for those workers who joined Walmart early enough and stayed long enough, the sums involved could be head-spinning. It wasn't unheard of for the individual profit-sharing accounts of longtime frontline workers to swell to hundreds of thousands of dollars. Some became millionaires. Even if profit sharing didn't make you rich, it could make things more agreeable. At the Walmart in Springdale, Arkansas, at least one worker took to sitting down once a year and figuring out what her profit sharing equaled on an hourly basis. And when "I was not making what I felt like was a decent wage," she said, this extra remuneration came out to 50 cents or a dollar an hour, "and that made it worthwhile." She wasn't alone. "Store associates are willing to work long years for modest pay and slim wage hikes," *Discount Store News* reported, "content on knowing they will hold small fortunes in Walmart stock upon retirement."

The other thing that seemed to keep many Walmart workers content was getting to interact with Walton, as a salesclerk in Monroe, Louisiana, articulated in verse:

Who is this man? The man they call Sam.
I would love to meet him and shake his hand.
He started with an idea and made it an empire
Through work and dedication, a man to admire.

Flying from store to store, Walton would show up wearing the same plastic name tag as his hourly employees, with "SAM" printed in capital letters, as if somebody might not know who he was. At store openings, he would lead employees in the company cheer, which, while striking some as hokey and strange, helped to foster an unmistakable esprit de corps: *Give me a W! Give me an A! Give me an L! Give me a squiggly!* (followed by a shaking of the butt) *Give me an M! Give me an A! Give me an R! Give me a T! What's that spell? Walmart! What's that spell? Walmart! Who's number one? The customer! Always!* "In headquarters, with his executives, Walton could be—and was—tough, blunt, and demanding," Ortega, the journalist, has written. "But on store visits, he was attentive and avuncular, getting hourly workers away from their managers to get their feedback." Said Carol Marang, who started at a Walmart in Guthrie, Oklahoma, in 1975: "He was always so nice and talked to you and listened to you like you were important."

Being attuned to his workers' concerns, Walton came to believe, was the best way to keep organized labor at bay—and he implored his managers to not just listen, but "listen aggressively." Under the paternalistic banner "We Care," Walmart rolled out an "open door" policy wherein workers were instructed that they could raise a grievance to any company manager, all the way up to Walton himself, without any fear of reprisal. "Anytime the employees at a company say they need a union, it's because management has done a lousy job of managing and working with their people," Walton posited. "Usually, it's directly traceable to what's going on at the line supervisor level—something stupid that some supervisor does, or something good he or she doesn't do." Whenever Walmart has had problems, said Walton, it was because store managers "weren't as open with their folks as they should have been. They didn't communicate with them, they didn't share with them."

In 1971, Walmart began publishing a monthly magazine, *Wal-Mart World*, as another avenue of communication with employees. Walton wrote a letter to his workers in each edition, never failing to thank them as the company blew through one sales and profit milestone after another. "I've been repeatedly asked...as to Walmart's secret," he wrote in May 1972. "Proudly, you're Walmart's 'secret,' and we frankly admit to it." In July 1974, there was this: "How does Walmart do it?...The answer is always the same—people. Not only the right kind, but interested, dedicated, enthusiastic, and loyal people. That's what makes our company exceptional, and what enables us to continually achieve the seemingly impossible." And in December 1978, this: "Let's don't ever forget—Walmart is a partnership. We're in this thing together. It's ours. We're all part of one fine company, and we have some future together as partners if we continue to work with and for one another!"

Nothing, however, cemented the company's mores quite like the corporate annual meeting in Bentonville. Year after year, Walton brought in busloads of workers, packing an auditorium and turning what could have been a dry and tedious affair into something that was part pep rally and part star-studded Las Vegas–style revue, complete with A-list entertainers and sports stars: Reba McEntire, Chet Atkins, Alan Thicke, Joe DiMaggio. "It's not really a corporate stockholders' meeting, is it?" Walton asked the crowd one year. "It's a happening—it's a revival!"

Standing behind the unremitting boosterism, meanwhile, was remarkable business acumen. Through the 1980s, with Walton having overcome his hesitancy to spend on technology,

Walmart knitted together an unrivaled logistics and distribution apparatus, which used barcodes, links between its computers and those of its suppliers, and a satellite system to keep tabs on every piece of merchandise as it moved from a factory to the company's trucking fleet to a cash register in the store. Armed with this insight, Walmart could fine-tune its ordering patterns in real time, based on what was selling and what wasn't, and keep its inventories lean. It could make sure that workers were ready to receive products as they arrived at the loading dock—and not be standing around, idle, whenever an 18-wheeler was running late. All of this saved money. For every dollar of goods sold, Kmart spent five cents on distribution; Walmart spent just two.

As the 1980s unfolded, Walmart rocketed ever further ahead. It broke out of its confines in and around the Ozarks, stretching into Arizona, New Mexico, Colorado, Michigan, and Wisconsin. By the end of the decade, it had 1,400 stores—more than a fivefold increase from 10 years earlier—along with 120 membership-only Sam's Wholesale Clubs, where shoppers could buy in bulk and find even greater savings. (Walton had appropriated the concept from industry pioneer Sol Price.) Because the average size of a Walmart had gotten bigger and bigger over the years, the workforce mushroomed at an even faster pace and now surpassed 275,000 employees—more than 10 times the number at the start of the '80s.

Yet even as the company exploded, it continued to execute superbly. In 1987, *Time* magazine hailed Sam Walton as "one of America's most restless and evangelical corporate leaders," adding that "thanks to his uncanny ability to motivate employees and slash expenses, the chain of discount stores Walton started just 25 years ago has become the fastest-growing and most influential force in the retailing industry." The report quoted a First Boston equity analyst as saying that Walmart was "the best-managed company I've ever followed, and I've looked at hundreds." Compared with other discounters, *Time* said, Walmart "offers more: well-scrubbed aisles, fully stocked shelves, and relentlessly upbeat clerks."

As the magazine lavished this praise, Walton was at the tail end of his run. The following year, fighting leukemia, he handed the reins to a new CEO, David Glass. Four years later, Walton passed away at age 74—just a month after he was awarded the Presidential Medal of Freedom, the nation's highest civilian honor. At the ceremony, President George H. W. Bush called him "an American original" who "embodies the entrepreneurial spirit and epitomizes the American dream."

Glass, whom Walton had lured away from the Consumers Markets grocery chain in 1976 to be his chief financial officer, had been instrumental in realizing that dream. Specifically, Walton gave his successor "the lion's share of the credit" for building out Walmart's enormously efficient automated distribution system. Like Walton, the New Liberty, Missouri, native was plainspoken, hard-charging, and steeped in the values of rural America. By all accounts, he was unfailingly humble. And he liked to hang out in stores, mingling with the troops, just like Mr. Sam did. But unlike Walton, Glass had little charm, at least in public. To many, said Ortega, "he could seem a bit of a stiff."

Yet whatever deficiencies Glass might have had, at least as measured against a figure as glorified as Sam Walton, they didn't slow Walmart down one bit. During his 12-year tenure as CEO, growth accelerated like never before. Glass bet big on

Supercenters, selling groceries alongside general merchandise inside cavernous new stores staffed by some 300 workers. Some questioned this thrust, given the low margins and brutal competition among supermarkets. But Glass didn't waver. "I've always been a proponent of one-stop shopping," he said. And before long, Walmart used its superior technology and supply-chain management capabilities to become an industry juggernaut.

In 1988, Walmart had two Supercenters. When Glass stepped down as CEO in 2000, there were more than 700 (as well as 1,800 Walmart discount stores, now in all 50 states and Puerto Rico; nearly 500 Sam's Clubs; and a presence in eight other countries). Sales had leapt from $16 billion to $165 billion—a track record that led McMillon to submit, without hyperbole, that "David Glass may be the most under-appreciated CEO in the history of business."

Walmart's next CEO, Lee Scott, picked right up where his predecessor had left off. By the end of 2003, Walmart had more than 1,400 Supercenters, doubling its footprint in the grocery business in just a few years. It was now the country's largest purveyor of food—bigger than Kroger or Safeway. Walmart's unmatchable low prices had also helped to send more than two dozen other supermarket chains into bankruptcy. They just couldn't keep up.

And it wasn't only in groceries where Walmart exerted substantial power. It was also America's largest seller of toys, furniture, jewelry, dog food, and scores of other consumer products. Having eclipsed Exxon Mobil, Walmart was now raking in more revenue than any other American company. Businesspeople everywhere looked on in awe. "For most of Walmart's 41 years, corporate America refused to acknowledge the retailer as one of its own," said *Fortune*, as it named Walmart the world's "most admired company" for 2003—the outcome of a survey of 10,000 executives, directors, and analysts across the globe. "Walmart was Podunk, USA, Jed Clampett, Uncle Jesse's pickup—and worse yet, a discount store. This year its transfiguration is complete."

But such accolades veiled the denunciation that had been mounting from other quarters for some time—from Main Street merchants Walmart had steamrolled, US manufacturers that Walmart had coerced into moving production overseas to lower costs, and human-rights watchdogs troubled by abuses abroad. David Glass had gotten one of the first tastes of such reproach in 1992 when he was confronted with hard evidence on *Dateline NBC* that child laborers in Bangladesh were sewing private-label clothing for Walmart, even though they were being sold on the rack as "Made in the USA." Informed that young girls had been locked in the factory overnight so that they had to keep working, Glass cracked. "Yeah," he said coldly, "there are tragic things that happen all over the world." With the cameras rolling, a Walmart public relations official abruptly ended the interview.

Walmart assailed *Dateline* for ambushing Glass and, it maintained, distorting the facts. More generally, as the vilification of the company intensified through the years, the brass in Bentonville reasoned that much of the contempt was an inevitable drawback of getting so big. "Because of the company's size and success," said Don Soderquist, who had become Walmart's chief operating officer, "it has become a lightning rod." He fretted that Walmart was being unfairly "judged on a standard of perfection" and that every stumble had "the potential to appear on the evening news or on the front page of the local paper," even though some missteps were to be expected with more than one million people now working for the company in the United States alone. "Can you imagine a city of one million people... that is held to a standard of zero mistakes by its citizens?" Soderquist asked. The heat that the company was suddenly feeling wasn't coming from nowhere, either. It was being fanned, Soderquist said, by other businesses that were looking to sully Walmart "rather than trying to compete" and labor organizers angling to make inroads at the company, or at least slow down its assault on unionized grocery chains, where the wage-and-benefit package was about $10 an hour higher. (The *Dateline* revelations had come courtesy of the United Food and Commercial Workers.)

But even if Soderquist had a fair point or two, it wasn't just outsiders with an agenda who were adamant that Walmart had veered off course. Employees who had been around since Mr. Sam's day began to complain that although Walton had built the company on two pillars—containing costs so that he could give customers the lowest possible prices while, at the same time, making his workers feel like he was good to them, even if wages were skimpy—Walmart had let the latter crumble away. It was now fixated almost exclusively on curtailing expenses. "Financial discipline," said Charles Fishman, who reported on Walmart for *Fast Company*, "had become for some an excuse for exploitation and mistreatment."

In dozens of stores, this would manifest in managers hounding employees to work off the clock through lunch and rest breaks. At a Walmart in Apple Valley, Minnesota, Nancy Braun wasn't even permitted to leave her post as the cook and waitress at the store's grill to go to the bathroom, although she had frequent urges after gallbladder surgery. "I'd get in a pinch, be there all alone, and soil myself, ruin my clothes," Braun said. "I'd feel so degraded. Sometimes I wouldn't have clothes with me, and the manager would say, 'We have clothes here for sale. Get your purse and go buy yourself some.' They didn't care."

Braun's humiliation was extreme. But across the country, the same dynamic was playing out over and over: Walmart higher-ups pushed those running the stores to rein in their payroll costs, prompting wage-and-hour violations. "This wasn't the case of a rogue manager here or there," said Jon Parritz, a Minneapolis attorney who represented Braun and about 100,000 other Walmart workers in a class-action lawsuit that ultimately was settled when the company agreed to pay more than $54 million. "The causes for this were systemic."

For many, it wasn't lost wages that bothered them; it was an awareness that they had lost something far greater. "The day Sam died was the day Walmart joined corporate America," said Kathleen MacDonald, who worked at a Supercenter in Aiken, South Carolina. "Things changed drastically." She said that where managers once solicited input from hourly employees, "the personable comments were put to a minimum, our ideas no longer respected. The way we felt about things was no longer considered." Marilynne Stanhope, who worked in the sporting goods department of the Walmart in Wasilla, Alaska, said the store had become so impersonal that "managers don't even know your name."

Under Sam Walton, "employee allegiance to the company's corporate culture...seemed to take on nearly cultlike proportions," wrote Sandra Vance and Roy Scott, two historians who documented Walmart's spectacular rise from the 1960s through the early 1990s. With Walton gone, the magic was fading, and that made the sting of low wages a lot less tolerable. At a Walmart in La Plata, Maryland, employees now balked at the company's signature ritual. "Half of us don't even do the cheer," said one worker. "Why should we, the kind of money we make?" By 2002, the vest that Barbara Ehrenreich had worn—the one that said, "Our people make the difference"—had given way to a new smock that said, "How may I help you?" For many, the switch encapsulated everything. "Walmart's great for the customers," a La Plata employee said. "But if you're an associate, it's a dog's life."

In 2003, the *Los Angeles Times* ran a three-part series that peeled back the paradox Walmart had become: a corporate colossus able to fulfill consumers' insatiable craving for low-price products, but at an increasingly high cost to its own workers. "Walmart gives," the lead article said. "And Walmart takes away."

My fingerprints were all over this one.

I am a journalist and business historian, disciplines that cherish detachment. But I can't make any pretense to being disconnected regarding Walmart.

I was the business editor of the *Los Angeles Times* when that 2003 series was published, and I had a large hand in shaping it. "Walmart's astonishing success exacts a heavy price," it affirmed. "By the company's own admission, a full-time worker might not be able to support a family on a Walmart paycheck." We would win the 2004 Pulitzer Prize for National Reporting for our appraisal of the retailer. My last book, *The End of Loyalty: The Rise and Fall of Good Jobs in America*, was even more pointed. It held up Walmart as a paragon of post-1970s capitalism, which has prioritized the interests of shareholders over employees. Many of Walmart's workers, I wrote, had been "placed on a path to impoverishment."

But in time, I'd start to see a different side of the company. The nonprofit social enterprise that I help to lead, the Drucker Institute, received funding in 2018 from Walmart's corporate foundation to develop a lifelong learning system through which residents of a local community could obtain new knowledge and skills. The company would eventually grant the institute $2.1 million—a good chunk of the $5 million that we'd raise for the project, which I've spearheaded. (Most of the additional money came from Google, as well as from public and private organizations in South Bend, Indiana, where our program got underway.)

When the Walmart funding first materialized, I couldn't get over it. The company obviously knew that I had been among its harshest detractors. But two Walmart executives had heard me give speeches about *The End of Loyalty*, which included a riff about the need in our fast-changing economy for robust worker training—something that most large companies once provided but that, like many parts of the corporate social contract, had melted away over the past 40 or 50 years. They approached me afterward and encouraged the Drucker Institute to apply for a grant for our then-nascent lifelong learning initiative.

Walmart's foundation, now called Walmart.org, has an unusual sense of kinship with the company. At many corporations, philanthropy is looked upon as an appendage. By contrast, executives from Walmart and Walmart.org routinely sit at the same table and collaborate. I was therefore able to meet senior managers who were helping to make key strategic decisions, not just dressing the windows.

As I got to know people at Walmart, I was surprised. Many were much more liberal in their politics than I'd anticipated. Some identified as progressive. A good half-dozen told me that they had thought of Walmart as "the evil empire" before they got there. But the recruiter persuaded them to come and listen. And once they set foot in Bentonville, it didn't take long to be swayed that Walmart was sincere about reforming many of its past practices, especially those pertaining to its frontline workers. This was an amazing chance, more than one told me, to change the world from the inside.

As these conversations continued, the more intrigued I became—and the more convinced that something meaningful was transpiring at Walmart. And so, I pitched the company: I wanted to tell the story of how it was transforming its relationship with its hourly workforce. And I was just the right person to do so. After all, who could be more credible than someone who had decried Walmart's conduct for so long?

All the while, I stressed that none of this would be possible unless I could pursue things on my own terms. For starters, I'd need complete and open access—something the company had never given a journalist before. For many years, it had batted down book proposals. When Bob Ortega tried to enlist Walmart's participation in the 1990s for what became *In Sam We Trust*, he was rejected straightaway. "Why should our busy executives take time away from their work for interviews," a

Walmart vice president pressed Ortega, who was then at the *Wall Street Journal*, "unless we have some reason to believe the book will either make our stock price or sales go up?" When Charles Fishman wrote 2006's *The Wal-Mart Effect*, he ran into similar resistance.

As much as I wanted Walmart to let me peek into its inner workings, I took pains to be straight-up. While I genuinely thought the company's ever-improving treatment of its hourly employees hadn't gotten the attention it deserved, and this book would be a way to rectify that, I wasn't going to pull any punches. I told the company that I'd be reaching out to its staunchest antagonists, including United for Respect, the United Food and Commercial Workers, and Senator Bernie Sanders, who'd introduced a bill that would prevent large companies from buying back their own stock (often to bid up the price) unless they paid all of their workers at least $15 an hour. The name of the legislation: the Stop WALMART Act. This would be no corporate hagiography.

I set some other parameters, as well. Walmart is in the thick of many issues—guns, opioids, and the injection of money into politics, to tick off just a few—for which it is sometimes lauded and other times lambasted. It is also vying with Amazon for retail supremacy, a battle of behemoths that undoubtedly colors just about everything Walmart does. Each of these topics is worthy of deep exploration in its own right. But while I'd touch on some of them, I'd keep my lens primarily on the state of Walmart's hourly workers.

In so doing, I hoped to shed light on some larger questions. Among them: Did Walmart's progress on wages signal a new chapter for American business in general? In recent years, more and more companies had renounced the principle that their only responsibility was to maximize their profits and share price. They vowed instead to be good stewards of their people and the planet, a swing in emphasis that went by any number of names: conscious capitalism, inclusive capitalism, stakeholder capitalism.

In October 2018, I was asked to attend a small dinner hosted by Jamie Dimon, the chief executive of JPMorgan Chase, who was then the chairman of the Business Roundtable, a lobbying group composed of the nation's leading CEOs. I'd been invited, along with a few other professional noodges, after I'd written an essay denouncing the Roundtable for its long-held stance that "the paramount duty of management and of boards of directors" was "to the corporation's stockholders" and that "the interests of other stakeholders" were "relevant," but only as "derivative" of this preeminent obligation. Ten months after our spirited dialogue with Dimon, and much to my amazement, the Roundtable yielded. It proclaimed that its members "share a fundamental commitment to all...stakeholders"—including their customers, employees, suppliers, and shareholders—and would "deliver value to all of them, for the future success of our companies, our communities, and our country." While hardly dead, the shareholder-über-alles mindset, promulgated most famously by economist Milton Friedman, was now on the defensive.

Walmart very much sees itself as part of this new wave of capitalism, talking up its adherence to "shared value," which calls upon companies to generate economic value in a way that simultaneously generates value for society by addressing its most urgent needs. "Walmart was an early mover and early leader in this way of thinking," said Michael Porter, a Harvard

Business School professor who is one of the fathers of shared value. In 2020, Dimon passed on the chairmanship of the Business Roundtable to McMillon, extolling him as "a forward-looking leader who understands the importance of a growing and inclusive economy that serves all Americans."

But what constitutes "inclusive"? With all that Walmart has done to make things better for its employees since 2015, are its jobs (or most of them, anyway) now "good" jobs? What does "good" even mean anymore? Are they "middle class" jobs? Does it make any sense to think that today's Walmart worker should attain comparable pay and benefits to, say, that of a General Motors worker in the 1950s?

McMillon has said that retail wages would probably go beyond $15 an hour in due time, and the federal wage floor—stuck at $7.25 since 2009—should be higher. "Do I think that the country should have been raising the federal minimum wage all along? Yes," he said. "Do I think we should have a catch-up right now to some number and then index it going forward" to match inflation? "Yes. Please do that." But McMillon also has advised that Congress should be careful to proceed at "the right pace" and take into account "geographic differences" and possible repercussions on small businesses.

Then again, why $15? Why is this presumed to be the right destination for tens of millions of low-paid workers around the country? The Service Employees International Union sparked the Fight for $15 movement back in 2012 with an initial strike by fast-food workers in New York City. But it isn't 2012 anymore. The median sales price of a home in the United States is 84 percent more now than it was then. Employees are spending 40 percent more for family health coverage. The cost of a four-year college is up about 20 percent. Do the math and you're compelled to ask: Shouldn't it be the Fight for $18 or maybe the Fight for $27 at this point? Besides, even if the cost of living had somehow held steady, $15 an hour is equal to about $30,000 a year—and that's for those able to cobble together enough work hours to be a full-time employee. Should aspiring to that threshold be seen in the richest country on Earth as a triumph or a travesty? (Some, with this perspective in mind, have started using the Twitter hashtag #Strivefor25, occasionally punctuated by #Fuck15.)

In early 2019, I traveled to Bentonville to make my case in person. Having taken shots at the company for so long, it felt more than a little odd to be walking through the doors of the Walmart Home Office.

"Did you ever think you'd be allowed inside here?" one of my hosts asked.

"Not alive," I replied, only half-joking.

After several months of back-and-forth, Walmart gave me the green light on the book. The company would cooperate.

I am not naive. Some are going to dismiss anything good that I have to say about Walmart as a requital for the millions of dollars the company has given to my institute. And I get why they might be skeptical. Corporations open their checkbooks "not only to mold the nature of criticism and pressure," as scholars Peter Dauvergne and Genevieve LeBaron have said, "but also to legitimize business growth" and "mute calls for stricter and more binding regulation."

My friend Dorian Warren, a political scientist and community organizer, fought against Walmart as it endeavored to expand into New York City in 2011 only to get a phone call out of the blue from a public affairs executive at the company. After some small talk, Warren said, the official asked if he'd like Walmart to fund his research on low-paid workers—a proposition that Warren, then a professor at Columbia University, deemed "a clever but cynical ploy to buy me off a little." He declined.

Many who have sought and accepted Walmart money for their organizations have done so with eyes wide open. Still, some can't help but wonder if taking any corporate dollars might lead them to self-censor. "Are we not saying as much as we should be saying out of fear of losing that funding?" asked Molly Kinder, a fellow at the Brookings Institution. In the pandemic's first year, Kinder castigated Walmart for not paying its frontline workers enough. "Companies like Walmart . . . have the means—and the moral imperative—to provide higher hourly hazard pay and raise wages permanently," she wrote in December 2020. Yet in a former position, when she was raising money directly from Walmart, it would have been trickier to be so outspoken. The study she was leading, which delved into what technological disruption portended for the future of work and workers, was being underwritten by Walmart. "It's subtle," Kinder said. "It was not that anyone told me not to do it. I just found myself less willing to say the stuff that I should have been saying."

As for myself, I can simply attest that I went into my examination of Walmart the same way I've always sized up a subject: with an open mind and a penchant for discerning the gray in things.

I sit shoulder to shoulder with progressive activists and union leaders on the boards of a farmworker trust and a publication called *Capital & Main*, which specializes in covering the scourge of income inequality. But I've also spent more time around business executives than many of my fellow travelers. At the Drucker Institute, where I was the founding executive director, we've held workshops and consulted with many big companies—Macy's, eBay, Coca-Cola, Verizon, and others—to help them become more innovative and better-managed from a holistic and humanistic standpoint. I've steadfastly subscribed to the view that business can be a force for good in the world.

In many respects, the man for whom the institute is named—the late Peter Drucker—has become my role model. Drucker was dubbed a "business guru," but he didn't gravitate toward business because he was interested in the ins and outs of commerce. He saw himself as a "social ecologist," intent on studying our "man-made environment the way the natural ecologist studies the biological environment." What captivated him was "the fact that the large corporation" had by the 1940s "become America's representative social institution."

"Even the most private of private enterprises," Drucker wrote in his 1954 landmark, *The Practice of Management*, "serves a social function." Drucker was no bleeding heart, however. A company's "first responsibility," he counseled, was "to operate at a profit" so that it could assume its rightful place as "the wealth-creating and wealth-producing organ of our society." But profit wasn't the only thing, or even the main thing, that a company should center on.

It must, first and foremost, meet its customers' needs, Drucker said, because it was "to supply the consumer that society entrusts wealth-producing resources to the business enterprise." A company also had to do right by its workers, or it might breed "class hatred and class warfare," which could well "make it impossible for the enterprise to operate at all." In the end, wrote Drucker, "what is most important is that management realize that it must consider the impact of every business policy and business action upon society. It has to consider whether the action is likely to promote the public good, to advance the basic beliefs of our society, to contribute to its stability, strength, and harmony."

As Drucker opined on the need to balance all of these responsibilities, he lived his life accordingly. Hanging side by side on a wall in his old house in Claremont, California—now a small private museum—are letters from two of Drucker's consulting clients. One is from Jack Welch, from when he was the CEO of General Electric. The other is from Cesar Chavez, the head of the United Farm Workers.

Drucker had always walked comfortably in the sometimes-conflicting worlds of management and labor. As he dug into General Motors for his 1946 book *Concept of the Corporation*, Drucker counted both GM President Charlie Wilson and United Auto Workers President Walter Reuther as friends. That case study—which, as Drucker summed it up, showcased the "workers' desire to be proud of their job and product" while entreating the company to "consider labor a resource rather than a cost"—left nobody happy. Most readers pigeonholed *Concept of the Corporation* as "strongly pro-GM and certainly pro-business," Drucker said, while those at the company regarded it as "an attack...as hostile as any ever mounted by the left." I love that. For the many years that I was a newspaper reporter, I reckoned that if I wrote about something contentious and vaguely pissed off both sides, I'd probably gotten it about right.

This isn't a very popular posture nowadays. America sees most everything in black and white. People and institutions are either good or bad—period. To call out some of both is to risk being written off as wishy-washy and weak, to be sneered at for capitulation and triangulation.

Many have lamented the death of facts in our country. I contend that we've also been afflicted by something equally dire: the death of nuance. (Nuance, my wife likes to remind me, doesn't get clicks.) "The world is messy," Barack Obama, who had his own dance with Walmart, has cautioned us. "There are ambiguities. People who do really good stuff have flaws." And there is this corollary: people and organizations that are deeply flawed sometimes do good stuff.

As to which of these framings would more accurately describe Walmart, I wasn't prepared yet to say. In early 2020, I was just trying to figure out why, in lifting its lowest wages, Walmart had gone down a road it had never before chosen to tread.

CHAPTER 2

Winds of Change

ONE OF THE first things you notice when walking into the Home Office in Bentonville is a large painting titled *Convoy*, which shows a fleet of tractor-trailers, most of them decked out with the Walmart logo, stretching down the highway as far as the eye can see. A police escort sits near the head of the procession, waiting to give the truckers permission to push through and make their deliveries. More so than in the news photograph from which the painting is derived, the foliage leans heavily over the road, as if sodden and wind-whipped. Gray clouds, some dark enough to feel a tad menacing, streak the blue sky. The little placard on the wall doesn't say exactly when or where this scene takes place, though it's safe to presume that most of those walking through Walmart's corporate doors already know. It is an image that, beyond any other, the company has used to define itself—or, more precisely, redefine itself.

In August 2005, the story goes, with Hurricane Katrina steadily gaining force, Walmart CEO Lee Scott set the tone for how he expected the company to react. The storm had just shifted westward and was now barreling toward the Mississippi and Louisiana coasts. "A lot of you are going to have to make decisions above your level," Scott told a roomful of company officers at their regular Friday meeting—three days before Katrina touched down. "Make the best decision that you can with the information that's available to you at the time, and, above all, do the right thing."

If there was any confusion about what Scott meant by doing the right thing, that was cleared up once Katrina made landfall, toppling telephone poles, ripping the roofs off buildings, flattening houses, and sweeping away entire communities. More than 1,800 people would lose their lives. As Walmart's senior executives gathered on a call, trying to figure out what to do, the talk turned to shipping bottles of water to hard-hit locations and taking other relatively modest actions—the things Walmart would typically offer up after a disaster. All of it would be helpful, certainly, but the aid being contemplated seemed small-bore given the devastation that Katrina had wrought. Scott interrupted.

"Hey, this is really bad, and it's getting worse," he said. He beseeched his team to think differently: "What if we stepped up big time?"

Doug McMillon, who was then running Sam's Club, said Scott's challenge was all that he and his colleagues needed. It was instantly apparent that the moment demanded far more than the company's usual solace. The norms of the business—including whether extending a hand might impinge on Walmart's profit-and-loss position—were to be jettisoned. "We saw it as an opportunity to throw the P&L to the side and throw everything at it: our people, our products, and our money," said McMillon, who now keeps a print of *Convoy* hanging in his office as CEO.

As for the people piece, Walmart workers became heroes. In Kenner, Louisiana, a company employee used a forklift to pry open the door of a warehouse and get fresh water to the stranded residents of a retirement home. In Waveland, Mississippi, an assistant manager drove a bulldozer through her flood-ravaged store so she could collect supplies and give them out to needy locals in the Walmart parking lot. Later, she broke into the store pharmacy to retrieve medicine to bring to the town hospital. In the heart of New Orleans, a company truck driver cut his way through downed tree limbs and navigated past the debris to reach a shelter filled with hurricane evacuees. As the throng spotted the Walmart name emblazoned on the side of the big rig, they jumped to their feet, clapped, and cheered.

In all, Walmart would haul some 2,000 truckloads of clothes and supplies to the areas that Katrina had pummeled—a stark contrast to the Federal Emergency Management Administration, which was largely paralyzed in the aftermath of the hurricane. By analyzing weather data, Walmart's in-house emergency operations center had helped the company to anticipate Katrina's magnitude. Its scale and expertise in logistics had then allowed it to answer the battered region's ensuing cries for help with great efficiency and effectiveness. Walmart gave out meals and medication to those who needed them but couldn't pay. It also won plaudits for giving cash advances and guaranteeing a job to every displaced employee. "If American government would have responded like Walmart has responded, we wouldn't be in this crisis," said Aaron Broussard, the president of Jefferson Parish, just south of New Orleans. Warren Riley of the New Orleans Police Department put it even more simply: "Walmart was our FEMA."

As the praise poured in, including from former Presidents Bill Clinton and George H. W. Bush, some couldn't help but question what was behind Walmart's display of compassion. After all, as historian Douglas Brinkley has written, for "a company often criticized as a money-grubbing monolith...the relief effort was a masterstroke of public relations." But despite the skeptics and cynics, for most of the general public and even the media, what counted in the end was not whether Walmart was self-interested in some way but that it had stepped up big time, just as Lee Scott had encouraged.

At the least, the company's exploits in the wake of Katrina likely caused a lot of people who had been convinced that Walmart was guilty of all sorts of iniquities to think again. "I feel like it started this conversation," said Brendan O'Connell, the artist who painted *Convoy*. "Is it possible that things are not as one-dimensional as we have perceived?"

O'Connell had been mesmerized by Walmart well before the hurricane struck, having always seen a kind of duality in the company. In 1999, he and his wife had moved from Manhattan to rural Connecticut, and he began hanging out at a Walmart in the town of Torrington. He'd later drop in on dozens of other Walmarts around the country. He loved the patterns and colors bursting forth from the packaging on the shelves—a boundless sea of commercialism—and he began to render Walmart's products and patrons in a series of works that has been compared to Andy Warhol's soup cans. But beyond the aesthetics, he was also intrigued by Walmart's push and pull on society. "Here's the most visited interior space on the planet," said O'Connell, referring to the 220 million consumers that Walmart attracts to its stores every week, "and yet culturally it's vilified." O'Connell has been careful not to turn his canvas into an editorial statement; he wants you to see whatever it is you see in Walmart, be it a company that is commendable or contemptible—or maybe a bit of both. "You know, Walmart is a huge place," O'Connell told me. "They do a lot of good things and a lot of not-so-good things."

For Lee Scott, Katrina was a chance to double down on the good. Two months after the hurricane, he appeared before a packed auditorium at the Home Office to give a speech that was to be beamed live to every one of the company's stores around the world, as well as to tens of thousands of its suppliers. No Walmart CEO had ever broadcast an address to such a wide audience, not even Mr. Sam.

Scott, who had started with the company in 1979 in the transportation department, had gotten to know Walmart a couple of years earlier as an outside vendor. He was working at the time for Yellow Freight, one of the nation's biggest trucking companies, and he had come to Bentonville to try to collect $7,000. David Glass, who was then Walmart's chief financial officer, wouldn't compromise on the payment, which Yellow Freight said was past due and Walmart disputed. But he was impressed by Scott's spunk, and he offered to make him manager of a Walmart distribution center. Scott turned him down flat. "I'm not the smartest guy that's ever been in your office," he told Glass, "but I'm not going to leave the fastest-growing trucking company in America to go to work for a company that can't pay a $7,000 bill." Undeterred, Glass kept after him until he accepted a job.

Like Glass and Sam Walton, Scott had unpretentious, small-town roots. Raised in Baxter Springs, Kansas, he worked through high school at his dad's gas station along Route 66. While in college at Pittsburg State, he held down a job on the night shift at a tire company, making steel molds. By his senior year, he was married with a baby and living in a 10-by-50-foot trailer close to campus.

He also shared at least two other traits with his CEO predecessors: First, he was a master at eliminating costs and expanding margins—something that he had demonstrated over and over as he climbed through the company, first in logistics and later in merchandising. And second, he was determined for Walmart to do whatever was required to stay ahead of its rivals, with one magazine profile taking note that "as Scott's star rose…the company churned out anti-Kmart lapel pins depicting a red K with a devil's face being choked or knocked out by the Walmart 'smiley.'"

But Scott also had a quality distinct from those who had come before him: a willingness to listen to Walmart's critics to a degree that they had not. Much of this was born of necessity. With the company under constant scrutiny and its reputation under assault—it was the subject of more than 2,000 news articles per week in 2004, compared with fewer than 1,000 in 2001—Walmart had no option other than to open up more to the outside world. Quoting a confidential survey, consultants brought in by the company warned that 2 to 8 percent of Walmart's customers had stopped shopping there because of "negative press they have heard." "Over the years, we have thought that we could sit in Bentonville, take care of customers, take care of associates, and the world would leave us alone," Scott said. "It just doesn't work that way anymore."

Whether Walmart was taking adequate care of its associates was highly debatable. And the company wasn't as guileless as it made itself out to be; the gee-whiz routine can be hard to swallow from the biggest company in America. Still, the basic point was valid. "We were so busy minding the store," Scott said, "that we didn't realize we had become a political symbol" until it was too late.

Most importantly, people inside and outside of Walmart have said that Scott, while he could be sarcastic and biting, gave real consideration to those who were pillorying Walmart for one thing or another. And he wanted his executives to let their guard down and do the same. On one occasion, Tom Mars, who joined Walmart's legal department in 2002 and became the company's general counsel, went with Scott to meet with a nun who was displeased with Walmart's wages and benefits for hourly workers. Just as Mars was about to walk through the door, Scott stopped him. "Hang on," he said. "Before you go in there, I'll tell you what your job is. Your job is to listen for that nugget, maybe two or three nuggets, but there will be at least a nugget of feedback that she's going to be absolutely right about. The big challenge when you're going into a meeting like this, Mars, is most of the criticism you're going to hear you're going to know is unfounded either because she doesn't know the facts or for some other reason. And so, for most people it becomes easy to treat this as an exercise in futility and go in there and smile and tune her out. But there's going to be something we can learn from this meeting. So that's your job." Included in Scott's personal list of 10 tips to succeed as a leader is this: "Harsh critics may be saying the very things you need to hear."

As Scott got ready to make his big speech to a live audience, one set of voices in particular had started to influence him: those of the environmental movement. They had found their way to Scott through Rob Walton, Sam's son and chairman of the Walmart board, who in 2003 had connected with the non-profit organization Conservation International. Peter Seligmann, CI's founder and chief executive, had at one point visited Bentonville at Walton's behest to give him and his siblings, nieces, and nephews an overview of different environmental causes. Seligmann said he went out of his way not to pitch CI but, rather, to help the Waltons understand "the significance of the challenge" and the "diversity of investments that could be made" with an array of environmental organizations—"from domestic issues to international issues, from brown issues to green issues." Lest there be any doubt about how much Mother Nature could use the support of America's richest family, Seligmann brought along a friend to underscore the incredibly high stakes: the famed naturalist E. O. Wilson, considered by many to be a latter-day Darwin.

Not long after, Rob Walton began accompanying Seligmann to Suriname, the Bird's Head Peninsula of Indonesia, and other spots to study marine and wildlife habitats. "We went all over the world looking at places so he could begin to listen and learn," Seligmann said. The most consequential trip was to Costa Rica, where Seligmann, Walton, Walton's son Ben, and another of Seligmann's friends, the Pearl Jam guitarist Stone Gossard, had been out diving for a couple of days. On their way back to San José to confer with top politicians and policymakers, they witnessed both the wonder and fragility of the sea: thousands of spinner dolphins danced off the side of their boat while a fleet of trawlers laden with the fins of sharks—dying out because of overfishing—passed by.

"Rob," Seligmann told Walton, "we're going to meet with the president of Costa Rica, and we're going to talk to him about securing the health of their oceans, and he's going to listen to me and he's going to think, 'NGO.' But if you speak up, he'll be thinking, 'market.' Are you willing to do that?" Walton said that he was.

Then Seligmann went in for the kill. "You know, no matter how much you do personally and how much your family does," he said, "the breakthrough is going to be when we can transform Walmart." On this, Walton demurred, flagging the fact that he was not an operating officer responsible for the day-to-day management of the business (even though he was chairman of the board and his family owned half of Walmart's stock). Prodded by his son, however, he gave in. "Okay," he said, "I'll introduce you to Lee Scott."

The CEO soon found himself in meetings with Seligmann and a couple of others, including Jib Ellison, a close friend of Seligmann's and a former river guide who had recently started up a management consultancy called Blue Skye based on a then-cutting-edge idea: that focusing on sustainability could provide big companies with a competitive advantage. Seligmann and Ellison told Scott that Walmart was the largest seller of farm-raised salmon in the world, that the pink color of

Walmart's salmon was from a dye—and that the coast of Chile, where the salmon was farmed, was now an ecological wasteland. Scott said that he had just had his first granddaughter and did not want Walmart to harm the Earth.

As the conversation turned to where Walmart might be vulnerable to environmental risks, Ellison tried to rejigger Scott's perspective. "With all due respect," Ellison said, "you're at risk everywhere because of your sheer size. You're exposed. However, Mr. Scott, there's a whole other way to look at this. It's not as a defensive strategy but much more as an offensive strategy building resilience into your business." After some more back and forth, Scott hired Blue Skye.

In September 2004, Ellison facilitated a two-day "choice meeting" for Scott, his most senior staff, and some of Walmart's most promising up-and-comers. The roster of participants had been finely tuned. "I spent weeks with Lee and Jib as Lee crossed out certain names I had suggested and added others," said Andy Ruben, Scott's head of strategy. "He was very focused on who was in the room." The group of 25 or so heard from Seligmann and other environmentalists on the precipitous decline of the world's natural resources due to global warming, pesticide use, and the depletion of fisheries. Scott was his caustic self: "Tell me why I should care about some endangered mouse in Arizona," he said, "when I just want to build a store." But Seligmann and Ellison didn't flinch, educating Scott and his lieutenants not only on the delicate balance of nature but also on how they could make money by diligently recycling and reducing waste. Now they were speaking Walmart's language.

At the end of the first day, "Scott told his executives that Walmart faced a decision," the journalist Edward Humes has recounted. "They could continue fighting the environmentalists and getting bad press and saying that the planet's deterioration was not Walmart's problem—that it was not our responsibility, not part of our core business. Or they could do what the environmentalists and Ellison had suggested and take on a leadership role in sustainability." Scott then took a vote on whether the company should move forward with a major new initiative on the environment. It was a unanimous yes.

Not everyone was completely sold, however. When Scott asked Ruben to lead sustainability alongside strategy, he said he'd need to chew on it. Ruben discussed the prospect with a few mentors, and they advised him not to take the job; it would be smarter to hold out and run a business unit, they said.

"That's just not a good career move for me," Ruben told Scott while the two were flying out for some store visits.

Scott peered over his bifocals. "My," he said to Ruben, then in his early 30s, "we're so young to think we know what's best for us." With that, the CEO went back to his crossword puzzle and didn't speak to Ruben while they were on the road for the next three days.

When they returned to Bentonville, Ruben walked into Scott's office and relented. "I think I'll do it," he said.

"I think that's wise," Scott said, without looking up. "Will you grab the door?"

In no time, Ruben was coordinating with managers to implement new sustainability objectives across just about every area of the business: energy, transportation, suppliers, waste, food and fiber, and packaging. Expert recommendations came from the Environmental Defense Fund, the Natural Resources Defense Council, the Rocky Mountain Institute, and others

Ellison had recruited. Some of the enviros were so nervous that "their constituencies would accuse them of collaborating with the enemy," as Humes described it, they swore Walmart to total secrecy.

From the start, the company discovered fairly straightforward ways to shrink packaging and retrofit its trucks to be more energy-efficient—quick, cost-saving measures that were in sync with its frugal culture. "The wins for Walmart in sustainability had paybacks," Ruben said. Following this low-hanging-fruit approach also helped to generate essential early momentum. "Little by little," said Humes, "one executive after another, then one department after another, began to look at their operations with different eyes, looking for the most efficient, least wasteful, more planet-friendly alternative."

Scott also remained intimately involved. In September 2005, a month before his speech, Ellison arranged for the CEO, Ruben, Environmental Defense Fund President Fred Krupp, and a professor of environmental studies at Brown University named Steve Hamburg to travel to New Hampshire's Mount Washington Observatory—at an elevation of more than 6,000 feet—to see firsthand how climate change was affecting the alpine ecosystem. Hamburg began by proffering a few academic insights, and Scott listened politely. But pretty soon, Scott cut him off.

"Look, Steve," he said, putting his hand on Hamburg's shoulder. "You wouldn't be here if you weren't a good scientist. But what I really want to talk about are the impacts of climate change on my customers and my company." Hamburg, smelling an opening, spent the next few hours exhorting Scott to change what Walmart carried in its stores, beginning with lighting.

Their exchange eventually led the company to commit to—and not only meet but exceed—what the *New York Times* said was a "wildly ambitious" goal: to sell in a single year 100 million compact fluorescent lightbulbs, each of which would use 75 percent less electricity, last 10 times longer, and produce 450 pounds fewer greenhouse gases in their lifetimes than the old-fashioned incandescent version. By 2011, Hamburg calculated, Walmart customers would be emitting 10 million tons less carbon dioxide per year than they otherwise would have, getting rid of the need for seven average-size power plants.

And so it was that, between Walmart's feats after Katrina and the company's environmental stirring, Scott had plenty to say in his speech. He just didn't know how to say it. For help, he turned to another unlikely source: Paul Hawken, who had been advocating for sustainable corporate practices for more than 30 years. Hawken was a businessman himself, having taken over the natural foods company Erewhon in 1967, soon after it was established. He then cofounded garden-tools retailer Smith & Hawken in 1979. But he was perhaps best known as a writer and activist.

Ruben had pulled Hawken into Walmart's orbit after reading his 1993 book, *The Ecology of Commerce.* It did not go easy on big companies like Walmart. "Some observers go so far as to suggest that multinationals *are* the 'nations' of the future," Hawken wrote. "Let us hope not, because there is a grave and crucial difference between a country and a corporation. Whereas the purpose of a corporation, as presently envisioned, is to grow and profit, the constitution of a country rarely begins or ends with such a narrow goal. Governments raise issues of social welfare, but corporations do not if it conflicts with their need to grow." And there was this: "Enormity, corporate or otherwise, has never been the friend of humankind." And this: "Business can provide meaning for workers and customers but not until it understands that the trust it undertakes and the growth it assumes are part of a larger covenant. As long as nature, children, women, and workers are abused by institutions espousing free-market theories, the *real* deficit will continue to grow—the difference between what business has taken and what it has returned, the difference between value added and value subtracted."

In some ways, Hawken stood out from the other outsiders whose advice Walmart was starting to heed because he had such a comprehensive view of what it took to be truly sustainable. He pressed Ruben, for example, to explore what it would look like if Walmart paid a living wage to all of its workers. "If we were not talking about a living wage," Ruben said, "Paul wasn't going to work with me on the environmental side." The way Hawken deciphered the world, "there really aren't environmental issues," Ruben pointed out. "They're all social issues."

By the time Scott reached out to Hawken regarding his upcoming speech, he had been through about 30 drafts—all of them thought by Walmart to be "drivel," as Hawken would remember it. "Finally, Lee called me up and said, 'Write the speech I should give.'" And Hawken did. "I wrote every word," he told me, "except the folksy intro and outro lines."

If the phrasing wasn't Scott's, the sentiments surely were. For the CEO, Ruben said, putting some real muscle behind sustainability was his single best shot at propelling Walmart "from an Arkansas company" into something much greater. From where Ruben sat, this was Scott's most daunting challenge as a leader. And to prevail, "he had to transform how the company saw itself, to change the narrative about who we were."

Scott began his speech by paying homage to Sam Walton and his inclination "to go where other businesses feared to go" so as "to help the people living in small towns and rural America enjoy a similar quality of life as those who lived in the big cities."

"In other words," Scott said, "we didn't get where we are today by being like everyone else and driving the middle of the road. We became Walmart by being different, radically different." Yet "even with this great beginning," Scott conceded, "we have received our share of criticism over numerous issues, not the least of which is our size." The CEO then laid out how he and other executives had spent a year listening to many of Walmart's critics. "You might be surprised about what we heard," Scott said. "Many of these individuals and groups see things differently than we do, but they also have ideas.

"After a year of listening," Scott continued, "the time has come to speak, to better define who we are in the world, and what leadership means for Walmart in the 21st century. Nothing brought this home more clearly than Hurricane Katrina. Katrina was a key personal moment for me.

"When Katrina hit last month, the world saw pictures of great suffering and misery. At Walmart, we didn't watch it, we experienced it. Some of our stores and clubs were underwater. Associates lost their savings, their homes, and in a few cases, their lives. I spent time with a few of them in the Houston Astrodome. I saw the pain, the difficulty, and the tears. But I saw something else. I saw a company utilize its people, resources, and scale to make a big and positive difference in people's lives....

"During this time, we were asked by governments, relief agencies, and communities to help. And look what happened. We were showered with gratitude, kindness, and acknowledgments. This was Walmart at its best.

"Katrina asked this critical question, and I want to ask it of you: What would it take for Walmart to be that company, at our best, all the time? What if we used our size and resources to make this country and this Earth an even better place for all of us: customers, associates, our children, and generations unborn? What would that mean? Could we do it? Is this consistent with our business model? What if the very things that many people criticize us for—our size and reach—became a trusted friend and ally to all, just as it did in Katrina?"

From there, Scott got more specific, putting forward three overarching goals for Walmart: to be supplied 100 percent by renewable energy, to create zero waste, and to sell products that sustain the company's resources and the environment. To help achieve these aims, Scott vowed that Walmart would, among other things, cut greenhouse gases at its existing stores and distribution centers by 20 percent over the next seven years; increase the fuel efficiency of its truck fleet by 25 percent over the next three years and double it within 10 years; reduce the solid waste from its US stores by 25 percent in the next three years; and favor suppliers, including those in China, that set their own substantial goals and lowered their own emissions.

And he didn't stop there. Scott said that Walmart would test out a new "community dialogue process" to fully address local needs and concerns when it built additional stores; take steps to ensure that its suppliers across the globe "support their workers by treating them properly"; and offer its own frontline employees more affordable health insurance, with premiums as low as $11 a month. He also said Walmart would become more transparent by regularly releasing statistics on the gender and racial composition of the company's workforce. The year before, a federal judge had granted class-action status in a lawsuit alleging that Walmart had systematically denied raises and promotions for female employees. The ruling created a class of up to 1.6 million current and former workers, making it the largest employment discrimination case against any company in US history.

And although Scott didn't go as far as Hawken wanted by pledging to pay a living wage at Walmart, he did say that the federal minimum wage—which had been languishing at $5.15 an hour for the better part of a decade—was "out of date," and he asked Congress "to take a responsible look" at raising it, along with "other legislation that may help working families." It was this wading into public policy, rare for Walmart at the time, that commanded most of the headlines.

"We are a large company," Scott said in conclusion. "For Walmart to be successful and continue to grow, we must operate in a world that is healthy and successful. Of course, we are acutely aware that we have a business to run, and run it we will. At the same time, we believe that these initiatives and many more to come will make us a more competitive and innovative company, and one that is more relevant to our customers....

"So again I ask," he said, "what would it take for Walmart to be that company—the one we were after Katrina: at our best, all the time?"

The question was inspiring, and Lee Scott was raring to show the world that Walmart had begun to fashion a compelling answer. The trouble was, he wasn't the only one telling Walmart stories. The unions were too.

If there is one thing that runs as deep in Walmart's DNA as its devotion to keeping costs down and prices low, it would have to be its antipathy toward organized labor.

The company's open-door policy, Sam Walton maintained, was the perfect avenue for hourly employees to bring any complaints they might have to management's attention, and he didn't want some third party wedging itself between Walmart and its workers. "We resent outsiders coming in and saying things which aren't true and trying to change the company that has meant so much to all of us," Walton said.

Whether Walton was also worried that a union contract would force him to pay his workers more, he never said. But whatever his mix of motives may have been, this much was certain: every time there was so much as a flicker of union activity at his company, Walton and his sidekicks would rush in and do everything they could to snuff it out.

Walton took his cues from attorney John Tate, who as a young man in 1936 had been conked on the head while crossing a picket line at Reynolds Tobacco Company in his hometown of Winston-Salem, North Carolina, where his father was a manager. It was a licking he never forgot. "I hate unions with a passion," he once said. An ardent conservative who construed his clashes with labor leaders as one aspect of a bigger fight for "freedom" being conducted by right-thinking Americans, Tate perfected the art of "union avoidance." By the early 1970s, when Sam Walton procured his services, Tate's bag of tricks included trying to keep workers happy by soliciting their input for improving the business and rewarding them with profit sharing. But he also had his clients trot out hardball tactics whenever necessary: convening captive meetings where workers were force-fed anti-union propaganda, delaying elections, stalling negotiations, replacing strikers, and moving to decertify unions that had won the right to represent the rank-and-file.

Walmart eagerly embraced all of Tate's teachings. When the Retail Clerks threatened to gain a foothold at two Missouri Walmarts in 1972, a company executive instructed the manager at one of them that if he caught any workers with union cards, he should fire them even if he had to bring on all new employees. When the Teamsters tried to organize a Walmart distribution center in Searcy, Arkansas, in 1982, Walton himself told the workers that he'd take away their profit sharing if they voted for the union. Then he went even further. "He told us that if the union got in, the warehouse would be closed," one of those in Searcy related. "He said people could vote any way they wanted, but he'd close her right up." All of this was illegal, but that didn't seem to give Walton any pause. The Teamsters lost the election, much to his delight. "Our good associates at our Searcy distribution center rejected the union by an overwhelming margin of three to one," Walton wrote in *Wal-Mart World*. "Bless them all."

For union organizers, attempting to penetrate Walmart was perpetually frustrating. When Mr. Sam was around, many hourly employees were persuaded that the company took sufficiently good care of them, particularly with profit sharing and the ability to purchase Walmart stock. "They felt they were going to be wealthy," said Pat O'Neill, who endeavored to organize Walmart workers in the upper Midwest for the United Food and Commercial Workers from the mid-1980s through the early '90s before later becoming a top union official. "It created a psychological barrier."

By the late '90s, Walmart had become so big, with hundreds and hundreds of Supercenters having been built in rapid succession all over the country, that there was almost no practical way for labor to make a dent. "It just started to blow up on us," said Ron Lind, a UFCW official in Northern California who suddenly had to deal with unionized grocery chains like Safeway and Kroger citing competition from Walmart as the rationale for holding down their own wages and benefits. An article in *Fortune* spelled it out like this: "Think your job is tough? Meet the people whose task is to unionize the world's biggest company."

Organizing Walmart store by store was essentially impossible because buttonholing workers across such a vast expanse entailed an equally vast expense—one beyond the capacity of any union or even group of unions. "If you tried to do the whole thing, it would cost a couple hundred million dollars," said Jeff Fiedler, a veteran UFCW organizer who, in an earlier post at the AFL-CIO's Food and Allied Service Trades Department in the 1980s, was the first person to sound the alarm for many of his union brethren that Walmart was on the verge of becoming a leviathan. And suppose organizers had been able to crack a few locations. So what? "It would be pure delusion to contend that a handful of isolated successes in individual Walmart stores would give workers significant power to bargain decent contracts with this giant, alien corporation," said Wade Rathke, a community organizer who tussled with Walmart on several fronts, including leading the resistance to the opening of new Supercenters in Florida.

Even isolated successes proved elusive, however. "I've never seen a company that will go to the lengths that Walmart goes to, to avoid a union," said Martin Levitt, who consulted with the company before writing a book called *Confessions of a Union Buster*. "They have zero tolerance." To gauge which stores were most susceptible to organizing, Walmart tracked employee attitudes and entered the results into a computer, which spit out a UPI—Union Probability Index. "The commitment to stay union free must exist at all levels of management—from the chairperson of the 'board' down to the frontline manager," read a manual circulated in 1991 at a Walmart distribution center in Indiana. "Therefore, no one in management is immune from carrying his or her 'own weight' in the union prevention effort." Whenever there was the slightest hint of an organizer coming around, salaried supervisors were directed to call a special hotline.

"We were basically spies, spies for the stores, spies for the company," said a department head at a Walmart in Kingman, Arizona, where the UFCW had made strides in organizing a group of auto technicians in 2000. A "labor team" from Bentonville was dispatched to the scene to monitor what was happening, coach management on how to defeat the UFCW, screen militant anti-union videos for the workers, and all but take over the store until the organization drive had been thwarted. Kingman wasn't an anomaly, either. Despite decades of trying—and the filing of 288 unfair labor practice charges against the company between 1998 and 2003 for purportedly surveilling, interrogating, and firing workers who hoped to organize—neither the UFCW nor any other union was ever able to notch a single victory at a Walmart in the United States.

Except for once. In February 2000, butchers at a Walmart Supercenter in Jacksonville, Texas, voted seven to three in favor of being represented by the UFCW. Soon, the company announced that it would stop cutting meat and instead sell prepackaged beef and pork at all of its stores. Walmart said this move to stock "case-ready" meat was long planned to keep pace with industry trends and that the UFCW's triumph was unrelated. In any event, Walmart was now able to argue that because the employees in Jacksonville were no longer using specialized meat-cutting skills on the job, they now failed to constitute an appropriate bargaining unit under labor law. The court agreed. Once again, Walmart had escaped being unionized.

In September 2004, right around the time that Lee Scott was holding his "choice meeting" on the environment, John Tate—then 86 years old and retired—was invited to speak to an assembly of Walmart executives and store managers in Dallas. "Labor unions are nothing but blood-sucking parasites living off the productive labor of people who work for a living!" he thundered. The Walmart faithful rose to their feet, hooting and shouting their approval. In the 1950s, Tate told the crowd, more than a third of all private-sector workers in the United States were union members. Now, fewer than 10 percent were. "Sam would have been proud of you for that!" Tate said amid another standing ovation. "The battle isn't yet won. I want to conclude by challenging you to reduce that percentage. You can do it and at the same time ensure your own future."

The unions weren't about to roll over, though. Far from it. About six months after Tate's provocation to Walmart managers, the UFCW and the Service Employees International Union both launched new campaigns against the company. Only this time, they were less about signing up workers and more about tearing down the company.

The SEIU kickstarted things in late 2004 when it seeded a nonprofit called the Center for Community and Corporate Ethics, which, in turn, stood up an advocacy arm known as Five Stones—a reference to the rocks that David plucked out of a streambed to slay Goliath. The Goliath in this case was Walmart, and the campaign designed to bring the company to its knees was christened Walmart Watch.

The SEIU's intention wasn't to drag Walmart to the bargaining table. Its membership was made up mostly of nursing aides, homecare and childcare workers, janitors, security guards, those in food services, and government employees; a retailer was beyond the union's purview. Rather, the SEIU set out to attack Walmart as if it were a political opponent—with nonstop negative messaging. "We referred to what we were doing as an air war," said Janet Shenk, who helped raise funds for the campaign. "We're not organizing workers on the ground. This is an air war."

Part of what the SEIU wanted to accomplish by going after Walmart so publicly was to raise people's consciousness about larger issues of economic justice that the union's president, Andy Stern, was increasingly upset about: income inequality, wage stagnation, and a dearth of good healthcare coverage for working people and their families. "This was a great way to get out there and say, 'Big corporations are screwing America,'" explained Stern, who led the SEIU from 1996 to the middle of 2010.

Walmart Watch also wanted to "make other businesses realize that if they act in the same irresponsible manner they will be attacked as well," according to an internal memo. Meanwhile, if Walmart could be bludgeoned into boosting workers' pay and benefits, other corporations were sure to follow suit. "It was never that they were absolutely the worst," Shenk said. "That's not why Walmart was picked on. It's because they were the biggest, and if they changed it would make a huge difference for the sector as a whole."

In April 2005, just as Walmart Watch was getting off the ground, the UFCW unveiled an analogous operation: Wake Up Walmart. But its desired endgame was different from the SEIU's. The UFCW, disheartened by how little headway it was making using traditional organizing methods, hoped that if it could rough up Walmart enough with a political-style broadside, the company might grow weary and agree to meet with the union. And if that happened, who could say where things would lead? Maybe UFCW representation, at least among Walmart's grocery workers, was possible after all. "Some people thought we wanted to put Walmart out of business," said Joe Hansen, the UFCW's president from 2004 to 2014. "We didn't want to do that. All we wanted to do was have a relationship with them."

Although Hansen and Stern respected each other and got along, the two anti-Walmart campaigns were at odds from the start. Bill McDonough, a UFCW executive vice president who was the architect of Wake Up Walmart, grumbled that mounting a public crusade against the company, to be staffed by political operatives, was his brainchild. Andy Stern, he said, "basically took our idea." Others inside the UFCW suspected that the

SEIU was longing to encroach upon the grocery industry and steal dues-paying members.

Those at Walmart Watch, for their part, groused that their Wake Up Walmart counterparts were trying to elbow them out of the way. They "told at least one print reporter to stop giving us so much attention" and "at least one television network we are not a 'legitimate' organization," said Andy Grossman, the executive director of Walmart Watch, when he alerted Stern in the summer of 2005. He also cautioned that the "open tension" was "causing tremendous confusion" among media outlets and the SEIU's allies, including a member of Congress whose office was leery of lending support because they didn't want "to get caught between UFCW and SEIU."

But if the unions could have made life even more difficult for Walmart had they cooperated, the internecine squabbling didn't matter much, if at all, to the company. From Walmart's vantage, the damage being inflicted was quite severe as it was. "We cannot directly undermine Walmart's consumer sales," a Walmart Watch planning document acknowledged. But "we can put them off-message; we can shape the message among the opinion makers they want to pursue; we can make them spend money on response; we can distract them through support of legal and legislative challenges."

For Grossman, who had been executive director of the Democratic Senatorial Campaign Committee, the move to Walmart Watch was an exciting diversion from politics. "I felt like Walmart was a drain on our economy in so many ways," he said. "It was the coolest thing to get to go take shots at the biggest company in the country. They were telling me to go hire the smartest people and apply these new campaign techniques to a corporate target." For others, however, Walmart Watch wasn't so much a departure from politics as an extension of it. "With the reelection of George W. Bush, we needed a new bad guy as a party," said Tracy Sefl, who had worked on John Kerry's presidential campaign and at the Democratic National Committee before becoming communications director at Walmart Watch. "Creating the fight around Walmart was perfectly timed. I felt from the start that we had a built-in constituency, and it was disaffected Democrats."

With several dozen staff members, Walmart Watch spent about $3 million a year thumping the company every which way. When the retailer tried to obtain a banking license, Walmart Watch sent a petition to federal regulators bearing 11,000 signatures opposing the application, helping to quash the company's plans. It teamed up with a group called Sprawl-Busters to assist local residents in towns across America who wanted to take up "site fights" and keep Walmart out of their communities. It helped to push legislation in Maryland under which any business with more than 10,000 workers would have to spend at least 8 percent of its payroll on employee healthcare—a measure commonly labeled the "Walmart bill" because it would have been the only company affected.

It promoted *Walmart: The High Cost of Low Price*, a scathing documentary by filmmaker Robert Greenwald, by pulling together thousands of showings at house parties, union halls, and churches. And it pounced on every Walmart miscue. When one of the company's hourly workers had been left brain-damaged after a tragic auto accident, Walmart tried to recoup hundreds of thousands of dollars in settlement funds, saying it had a fiduciary duty to recover the money on behalf of all employees in its health plan. The incident was a PR fiasco, and Walmart Watch, casting itself as guardian angel, created a donation page to help the victim.

It also ran big, splashy ads in the *New York Times*, including "A Handshake with Sam," which called upon Walmart to live up to Sam Walton's vision that "free enterprise" should be "practiced correctly and morally." Walmart Watch insisted that this was "an agreement proposed in good faith" to the company, though it came across as more of a gimmick. The ad goaded Walmart to fulfill its "moral responsibilities" by making sure "that employees are never mistreated" through intimidation, sexual harassment, or off-the-clock work violations; "paying a family-sustaining wage"; providing "quality affordable health insurance" to every full-timer and part-timer; and meeting a string of other obligations. It then asked people to visit WalmartWatch.com and urge the company to follow through—all part of compiling a digital list of the like-minded that, at this point, was still somewhat new to politics and even newer in terms of taking on a corporation.

In June 2005, Walmart Watch deployed more technology from the field of politics: an automated phone system that rang up 10,000 people in Arkansas and asked them to share any juicy secrets they had about Walmart. It's not clear if anyone responded to the robocall. But what happened several months later would become, for many who were part of Walmart Watch, the highlight of the campaign. It presented itself in a brown manila envelope with no return address.

The package landed on Grossman's desk at his office in Washington, and as was his custom, he shoved it in a stack of reading to take home. Plowing through the pile late that night, with his kids fast asleep, he pulled out the contents and couldn't believe what he saw. An anonymous source had sent a confidential analysis, originally put together for Walmart's board, that proposed various ways to lower the company's healthcare and benefit costs.

Written by a Walmart executive vice president, Susan Chambers, it outlined a number of "bold steps" that could help the company get a handle on these expenses, which were skyrocketing at the retailer just as they were at most other big employers. Included among the suggestions, which were assembled by a 15-person team drawn from across Walmart, were some that, as Grossman immediately recognized, would put the company right where he wanted it if they ever got out: in a terrible light. For example, one potential solution was to make jobs more physically demanding—such as by having cashiers gather shopping carts—so as "to dissuade unhealthy people from coming to work at Walmart." The memo also raised the specter of hiring more part-time employees and making cutbacks to the company's profit-sharing and retirement savings programs.

What's more, the document revealed that, on average, Walmart employees were spending 8 percent of their income on healthcare for themselves and their families—nearly twice the national average—and 46 percent of workers' children were uninsured or on Medicaid. While Chambers told the board that the company's "increasingly well-funded and well-organized critics" were not being fair in everything they said about the company's medical benefits, they "are correct in some of their observations." "Specifically," she said, "our coverage is expensive for low-income families, and Walmart has a significant percentage of associates and their children on public assistance."

The analysis also implied that—at least in raw economic terms—longer-serving Walmart workers weren't worth it. "The cost of an associate with seven years of tenure," it said, "is almost 55 percent more than the cost of an associate with one year of tenure, yet there is no difference in his or her productivity." In addition, Chambers wrote, what was "most troubling" was that "the least healthy, least productive associates are more satisfied with their benefits than other segments and are interested in longer careers with Walmart."

The next morning, Grossman pulled Sefl aside. "Hey, can you read this?" he asked. "I think there's really something here."

Sefl said she'd get to it ASAP—but then added the memo to her own mountain of reading. A couple of days later, Grossman reminded her to please take a look. This time, she did.

"Wow," she told him. "This is it."

At first, there was debate about whether leaking the document could backfire. Some at Walmart Watch were anxious that people might question how they got hold of something so sensitive. "Then it would become about us and not about them," Sefl said.

But she quickly dispensed with those apprehensions. "Fuck that," Sefl told the others. "Let's go big."

And they did, giving the document to the *New York Times*. The staging was impeccable, with the newspaper's story—"Walmart Memo Suggests Ways to Cut Employee Benefit Costs"—published just two days after Lee Scott had asked in his speech, "What would it take for Walmart to be...at our best, all the time?"

Chambers defended what she had written, saying that the emphasis was not on paring down costs but on giving workers more and better choices of benefits, like Health Savings Accounts. She also called the company's current health coverage "generous," telling the board: "It is important to note that our offering and performance are on par with other retailers; Walmart's critics, however, hold it to a 'large company' standard, not a retailer standard. Despite the difference in industry economics, critics believe we should behave more like a GM or a Microsoft than a Target or a Sears."

The additional context mattered not at all. A torrent of other disapproving stories followed the article in the *Times*. "An internal memorandum at Walmart," MarketWatch reported, "appears to contradict the spirit of change and benevolence" being ballyhooed by the company. The *Los Angeles Times* wrote that while Walmart "has talked a lot lately about becoming a kinder, more responsible company," it is "finding that convincing the world that it is 'committed to change,' and to keeping costs low, is a tough balancing act." Paul Argenti, a scholar of corporate communications at Dartmouth College, told NPR that Walmart had been "doing a great job" in showing themselves to be more "employee-oriented, customer-oriented, all of those things"—but now they had stepped in it. "This is going to set them back," Argenti said. "There's no doubt about it."

For any company, withstanding the continual fire from a campaign like Walmart Watch would have been a tall order. But Walmart also had to weather the second part of the unions' salvo: Wake Up Walmart. The UFCW didn't spend as much money on its parallel campaign as the SEIU did on Walmart Watch. But what it lacked in resources, Wake Up Walmart more than made up for in resourcefulness. "We were young and scrappy," said Buffy Wicks, who signed on to Wake Up Walmart after serving as an organizer for Howard Dean's 2004 presidential bid. Company executives would go on to give her a moniker in recognition of the formidable foe that she, along with her compatriots, turned out to be: "Buffy the Walmart Slayer." Two of the others who ran Wake Up Walmart were also refugees from the Dean camp. Another had been a top adviser to a different presidential hopeful, General Wesley Clark, while the final member of the team had worked in digital operations for John Kerry's campaign.

For Wicks, whose first exposure to activism came when she mobilized against the Iraq War in the Bay Area of California, going after Walmart was a seamless expression of her progressive politics. "It just felt like this was a very righteous cause," she said. Wake Up Walmart's Jeremy Bird, who had graduated from Harvard Divinity School in 2002 before knocking on doors for Howard Dean, was similarly motivated. But in his case, there was an added incentive to embarrass Walmart: "I knew about how they treated my mom when I was a kid," he said.

Jeremy's mother, Debbie Bird, who raised her family in a trailer park in High Ridge, Missouri, had helped open the Walmart up the road in Fenton in 1986. During the few years she was with the company, selling bedding, curtains, and furniture, she liked many things about it. She took pride in her work. "I was good at what I did," she said. "I made customers happy." The pay, a hair above minimum wage, was fine with her, especially with profit sharing included. When Sam Walton visited the store, chatting up Debbie and her coworkers, she found him enchanting. But as time wore on, Debbie began to speak out against certain practices, including the way some workers were having their schedules jerked around. "I got good reviews until I started saying, 'Hey, this isn't right,'" she recalled. Jeremy would never forget how his mother had been passed over for promotion to a salaried manager's position. "It always left a bad taste in her mouth," he said. Her worst day was when she threw out her back at the store and could barely move, but her manager wouldn't let her go home. When her workday finally ended and she returned to the trailer, aching and throbbing, she had to be helped out of the car. "Those are the kinds of things kids remember," she said.

As it kicked into gear, Wake Up Walmart relied on much of the playbook that Walmart Watch used. It ran newspaper and TV ads blasting Walmart. It helped to publicize and screen the Greenwald documentary slamming the company. It agitated for state legislation mandating that "large, profitable companies, like Walmart, pay their fair share for healthcare." It, too, got its hands on and leaked a corporate document—this one indicating that Walmart employees who were unwilling to work during the busiest evening and weekend shifts could wind up with fewer hours or drop to part-time from full-time. (This discovery didn't have nearly the same oomph as did the Susan Chambers memo on keeping healthcare costs in check.) And it signed up supporters—more than 200,000 in its first year, leading the director of Wake Up Walmart, Paul Blank, to declare it "one of America's fastest growing political and social movements."

But Wake Up Walmart also possessed a blend of creativity and pugnaciousness that set it apart. Some 22,000 people signed its "Love Mom, Not Walmart" pledge to not buy a Mother's Day gift at the retailer until it "addressed its record of discriminating against two million women." Its "Send Walmart Back to School" blitz, in partnership with two teachers' unions, asked Americans not to buy their school supplies from Walmart "until the company becomes a more responsible corporate citizen." Its "Nothing's Scarier Than Not Having Healthcare" drive, set for Halloween, included candy fundraisers in more than 90 cities to raise money for Walmart workers straining to pay their medical bills.

And then there was the campaign's most ingenious maneuver—the Wake Up Walmart bus tour. For 35 days beginning on August 1, 2006, and ending on Labor Day, Wicks, Bird, and four other Wake Up Walmart staffers rumbled into 35 different cities across 19 states aboard a 55-foot-long coach wrapped in red, white, and blue and bedecked with several calls to action: "Join America's Fight for Healthcare," "Join America's Fight for Good Jobs," and "Join the Fight for a Better America." Each night, two of the crew would rotate into hotel rooms for a shower and a good night's sleep; the others would snooze on the bus in tiny bunks, stacked three high. "We were trying to do a lot with very little," Bird said. The start of the tour couldn't have been more inauspicious. The bus, nicknamed Smiley, broke down on the very first day between Washington and New York. The driver wasn't so hot, either. With a gaggle of reporters standing there, he bounded off the bus in the middle of the first stop, barefoot and shirtless, puffing away on a cigarette. "He'd driven all these hair metal bands in the '80s and '90s," Wicks said. "We had to talk to him and be like, 'Okay, you've got to wear shoes and a shirt when we're at events, you know?'"

Once things got rolling, though, it couldn't have gone better from Wake Up Walmart's point of view. Thousands of people across the country turned out to listen to a litany of Walmart's sins through a presentation called "A Costly Truth," an echo of Al Gore's recently released film about global warming, *An*

Inconvenient Truth. Democratic politicians, hoping to score points with their base, showed up to stoke the crowd. Among those who took part were Senators Joe Biden and Harry Reid, as well as Governors Tom Vilsack and Bill Richardson.

At a plaza in Bridgeport, Connecticut, both Senator Joseph Lieberman and his primary challenger, Ned Lamont, made their way to the Wake Up Walmart rally in Smiley's shadow. Trashing Walmart, it seemed, was the only thing they could agree on. "As you might tell from the galaxy of signs out there, there's a political campaign going on," Lieberman roared. "But here's the great news: we're all together today in wanting to wake up Walmart and say, 'Treat your workers fairly.'" John Edwards, the former senator from North Carolina and 2004 vice presidential candidate who in the coming months would announce his own 2008 run for the presidency, met with the Wake Up Walmart bus in Pittsburgh and bashed the retailer for shunting so many of its workers onto the public dole. "It's not right and we all know it's not right," he said. "This is about responsibility and it's about basic human morality."

Walmart did its best to downplay the bus tour, dismissing it as "a union-funded publicity stunt." But the unrelenting onslaught from both Wake Up Walmart and Walmart Watch had, without question, succeeded in making the company "nearly as infamous as Enron or the Triangle Shirtwaist Factory," as *Salon* magazine characterized it. Lee Scott called the unions' barrage "one of the most organized, most sophisticated, most expensive corporate campaigns" ever waged. No longer, though, was Walmart going to just sit there and get pounded. The week before the UFCW bus took to the road, the company fortified itself and prepared to hit back hard.

CHAPTER 3

The Missing Link

LESLIE DACH, ONE of America's great spin doctors, was already well-acquainted with Walmart when he was tapped to join the company.

Over the previous year, he had led the Walmart account as vice chairman of Edelman, the public relations firm, which had been brought on by the retailer to stem the thrashing it was taking from the unions. But becoming a full-fledged Walmarter elevated Dach's authority—and formalized one of the more incongruous relationships in Lee Scott's universe.

Born and raised in Queens as the son of Holocaust survivors, Dach had earned degrees from Yale and Harvard and worked at the Environmental Defense Fund and the National Audubon Society. Captivated by politics, he became part of the advance team for Senator Edward Kennedy's 1980 challenge to the incumbent president, Jimmy Carter—a race in which Kennedy ran as a lion of New Deal liberalism. Dach went on to be an adviser for Democrats in four of the next six presidential election cycles, including managing the Democratic convention program for Al Gore in 2000. But his day job was flackery in the private sector, having begun a 17-year stint at Edelman in 1989.

Although Dach's politics were far to the left of Scott's, Dach was no stranger to joining ranks with those who held different values. At Edelman, he had worked hand in hand with Michael Deaver, who'd molded Ronald Reagan's political persona. Dach and Scott were also kindred spirits in enough ways that they came to appreciate one another. "I'm a troublemaker, and he's a troublemaker," Dach said. "He's sarcastic, and I'm sarcastic. He'd give me shit, and I'd give him—you know, respectful shit." Although there was a playful element to all of this, Dach became an asset in no small part because he would shoot straight with Scott in ways that some at Walmart wouldn't. Unlike them, Dach had no designs to get ahead; without any credentials in retailing, he wasn't going to be the next CEO of Walmart, and so there was no reason to sugarcoat things. "I have one job here," he said. "I'm not getting another one."

For Dach, who commuted between Washington and Bentonville, the hardest part of taking a job at Walmart was seeing the reaction of those in his political circles. "Thank God you're Jewish because if you were a Catholic, you'd be in confession 24 hours a day," Dach's good friend John Podesta, who had served as President Bill Clinton's chief of staff, told him. Union officials, many of whom had worked with Dach on one presidential campaign or another, disparaged him. "The only thing I can hope is he is doing it for the money because the Leslie Dach I knew wouldn't be there," said Joe Trippi, Howard Dean's former campaign manager who had produced a TV spot for Wake Up Walmart.

To his credit, Dach never denied that the money was good. His starting compensation package alone was worth $3 million, plus a heap of stock options. "It was more than I'd ever made in my life," he told me. But he also believed that the job was good—a welcome chance not only to further Walmart's environmental gains but to make big contributions in other areas. "I'm convinced Walmart is changing and the change is real," he said in announcing his move.

Actually, not all of it was real. While he was still at Edelman, Dach had helped start a pro-company group called Working Families for Walmart. Yet while the organization billed itself as "grassroots," it was anything but. Walmart funded Working Families, which was housed in Edelman's Washington offices. Members of its steering committee had business ties to the company. And a Working Families blogger, who drove around in an RV and posted stories of happy Walmart workers, was the sister of an Edelman executive.

The astroturfing, which was uncovered by the media and for which Walmart and Edelman were roundly ridiculed, was one piece of a bigger effort to neutralize the unions. Under the direction of Dach and Deaver, the company set up a rapid-response war room in Bentonville, which was named Action Alley. Staffed by their own team of political operatives, including top aides from the 2004 Bush and Kerry campaigns, they tried to get out in front of Walmart Watch and Wake Up Walmart by sponsoring events in which a lineup of company surrogates would speak in the same city where one of the unions was about to try to throttle the retailer. Dach and Edelman also ginned up TV ads to parry what the UFCW and SEIU were doing. Said one: "Our low prices save the average working family $2,300, a year. Which buys a lot of things—and a whole lot of freedom." When they needed to sling mud, they did that too. Working Families for Walmart put up a website called Paidcritics.com to impugn the integrity of the unions' leaders, claiming, for instance, that Andy Grossman of Walmart Watch had "a checkered past." (Wake Up Walmart retaliated with a new website of its own: www.abunchofgreedyrightwingliars whoworkforwalmart.com.)

But to make it seem that such gamesmanship was all Dach brought to Walmart is to turn him, unfairly and inaccurately, into a caricature. More than anything, he impressed upon Scott that the only way to mend Walmart's reputation was to "be a better company, not just do a better job telling your story," as the retailer had tried to do in early 2005 by running more than 100 full-page newspaper ads across the country, in what *Time* magazine designated a "charm offensive." At Edelman, Dach said, he'd counseled countless corporations that would "whine and complain and basically say, 'We're misunderstood.'" And there were a good many executives at Walmart who'd adopted the same woe-is-me mentality. Mona Williams, the company's vice president of corporate communications, sounded particularly aggrieved. "So much of the negative criticism is simply inaccurate that it hurts our feelings," she said. Dach made it his job to try to help Walmart get beyond this trope. And he had high hopes that it could, what with Scott's openness to shaking things up and what both men saw as Walmart's unique strong suit in being able to help the world: its gargantuan size.

In this, Dach knew they'd be cutting against the grain, as Americans have long been troubled by big corporations wielding exorbitant power. More than a century before Amazon, Apple, Facebook, and Google were said to have engaged in all manner of anti-competitive behavior, Louis Brandeis condemned "a curse of bigness" that had gripped the nation's financial arena, then controlled by J.P. Morgan & Company and a couple of other New York banks. These firms, the future Supreme Court justice avowed, had inserted their tentacles into myriad industries—coal, steel, electrical equipment, the railroads, and more—abetting corporate concentration across the country. Although laissez-faire capitalists celebrated this building up of ever larger enterprises as a mark of progress, the survival of the fittest, a natural evolution that would bring about a stronger society, Brandeis put forth that monopolies, oligopolies, and trusts were stifling innovation, foisting "extortionate prices" on consumers, and extracting "excessive profits." And that was the least of it. Tim Wu, a Columbia University law professor and a torchbearer today for vigorous antitrust enforcement, has explained that "Brandeis saw an economy dominated by giant corporations as tending to a certain inhumanity. He feared that working in a giant corporation might rob the American people of their character."

Large retailers and grocery stores were met with their own backlash in the 1920s and '30s, as federal and state legislators took on what *The Nation* magazine called the "chain store menace." The Great Atlantic & Pacific Tea Company, excoriated by a prosecutor in Franklin Roosevelt's administration as "a gigantic bloodsucker," was often in their crosshairs. In 1946, A&P was found guilty by a federal judge of violating the Sherman Antitrust Act. But the verdict was a twist on any conventional understanding of market manipulation. A&P's crime wasn't keeping prices artificially high, harming shoppers; it was making them artificially low, harming smaller businesses that were trying to compete. "We would rather sell 200 pounds of butter at one-cent profit than 100 pounds at two-cents profit," the company's president, John Hartford, had testified during the trial. In that sense, the historian Marc Levinson has asserted, "A&P was Walmart long before there was Walmart."

In fact, flash forward 50 or 60 years and Walmart would find itself trying to fend off similar accusations. One study concluded that the company impaired local economies by causing some small towns to lose as much as 47 percent of their retail trade within a decade of a Supercenter moving into an area. Others cited decreasing profit margins at nearby supermarkets, diminished retail employment overall, and a rising number of lower-paying jobs. The scholarship was far from unanimous on any of this; other researchers found that Walmart had a positive effect on local economies. Others said that, either way, the impact was negligible.

Dach's plan was to add on to what Scott was already doing and leave no doubt that Walmart's size and market power could be an unalloyed boon for America, flipping the "curse of bigness" on its head. Between Walmart Watch and Wake Up Walmart, the unions "had their feet on our neck, and they didn't want to let us up off the ground," Dach said. The only way to wriggle free was "to do things so big and so meaningful that even our harshest critics had to acknowledge that no one else was doing that."

For instance, Walmart cut the price of some generic drugs sold at its pharmacies to $4 for a 30-day supply in what it said was "a positive business move," as well as "a significant social benefit." A study in the *Journal of Health Economics* found that being able to access these cheap drugs made a real difference, improving the utilization of antihypertensive medications by 7 percent and decreasing the probability of an avoidable hospitalization by about 6 percent. Walmart also began distributing food to food banks and, in time, increased its donations from millions of pounds to billions of pounds. "Hunger is just a huge problem, and as the largest grocer in the country, we need to be at the head of the pack in doing something about it," said Margaret McKenna, the president of Walmart's charitable foundation. And it continued to plug away on the environment, blocking out "quick wins," longer-term "innovation projects," and "big game-changers" across all facets of the business. Along the way, Walmart pulled some of the most incredulous members of the green movement onto the company's side.

One of them was Adam Werbach, who in 1996, at the age of 23, had become the youngest president in the history of the Sierra Club. The next year, he published a book in which he called Walmart "a new breed of toxin." But in 2006, he agreed to consult with the company. "I wholeheartedly believe in what Walmart's doing, which astounds me," Werbach said. Regardless of whether "you love or hate Walmart," he added, "it has done more for sustainability than any environmental organization I've ever worked for."

It took Walmart longer to win over Jeffrey Hollender—but it did. The cofounder of Seventh Generation used to say that "hell would freeze over" before Walmart would be permitted to sell any of his company's environmentally friendly household goods. "We might sell a lot more products in giant mass-market outlets," he said, "but we're not living up to our own values and helping the world get to a better place if we sell our soul to do it." Hollender felt that Walmart's "tattered relationship with labor unions was a fundamental problem" and that the company needed to be much clearer with the public about its sustainability agenda and outcomes. Its "opaque, self-congratulatory website" wouldn't cut it. "You can't produce or sell anything without leaving some trace behind," Hollender wrote in his 2004 book, *What Matters Most*, a copy of which Lee Scott kept on his desk (right alongside *Sowbelly: The Obsessive Quest for the World-Record Largemouth Bass*). "But the most important thing is to fairly acknowledge and disclose the adverse effects that you do generate, and then take action to ameliorate them. A business should be willing to be held accountable to achieving measurable progress toward a predefined goal."

In late 2005, Hollender flew to Bentonville to talk with Scott and other high-ranking executives. "I was quite amazed that the whole senior management team showed up to meet with me when I was unwilling to do business with them," he said. Once in the room, he was taken aback all the more. "I was very critical of them, and they were eager to hear that criticism," Hollender said. "There was some genuine humbleness that I was sort of unprepared for. I thought I was going to do battle. And I met a group of people who didn't totally understand, but were eager to learn" about Seventh Generation's objections.

In due course, Hollender came around, and Seventh Generation began selling into Walmart. Although the company's conduct was "far from unblemished," Hollender said, "it's... wrong for us to essentially boycott a retailer that is working hard to improve." Hollender's thinking was also impacted by a Seventh Generation analysis, which looked at 16 labor, social, and environmental metrics at 18 retailers and supermarket companies. It showed that Walmart was no worse, and in some cases better, than its peers. "It didn't mean they were good," Hollender said. "But it was not really fair of us to refuse to do business with them and to do business with other of their competitors who had inferior practices." As the years went on, Hollender became ever more confident that Walmart was "putting increasing distance between what it once was and what it's becoming." One of Seventh Generation's "own corporate responsibility experts, someone who knows a poseur when he sees one, even suggests that Walmart has become a legitimate sustainability leader," he noted.

In the summer of 2006, Walmart landed its most prized convert: Al Gore. After *An Inconvenient Truth* was shown to about 800 Walmart employees at the Home Office, the former vice president and his wife, Tipper, sprang onto the stage to a standing ovation. "The message from Walmart today to the rest of the business community is, there need not be any conflict between the environment and the economy," Gore said. He quoted scripture and likened what Walmart was doing to the Allies' victory during World War II. "By taking this climate crisis on frontally and making this commitment," Gore said, "you will gain the moral authority and vision as an organization to take on many great challenges."

Not everything that Walmart has attempted to be more socially responsible on has panned out, including what could have been its most far-reaching accomplishment. Early on, the company planned to introduce to the world a 0–100 scoring system by which consumers could see at a glance how any product stacked up in three areas: sustainability, health, and social factors, including the manufacturer's wages and labor conditions. Red would signal that the item was below average for the industry, green above. More details—on, say, the amount of energy used, waste generated, and miles traversed to bring that product to the shelf—would be available by swiping a barcode on the tag with a cell phone. But the project, which environmentalists greeted as "a blockbuster for ecological transparency" that "could literally change the face of retail forever," never got very far. Stymied by the cost and complexity, the index creators decided instead to put sustainability information into the hands of corporate buyers, not regular customers. And even that system, while having been built out extensively, has only been used by Walmart to a limited extent. "It's just not a priority that gets brought into the buying room for the most part," said Jon Johnson, a professor at the University of Arkansas Sam M. Walton College of Business, who has helped to lead the program from the beginning. "It just hasn't happened as quickly as I would have hoped for."

Through the years, even as Walmart has met noteworthy sustainability goals and then set far loftier ones, some in the environmental community have continued to find fault with the retailer. Earth.org has identified Walmart as one of "12 major companies responsible for deforestation." Greenpeace has likewise accused Walmart of making "broken pledges" to protect forests, as well as relying on loophole-filled, third-party certifications in procuring seafood sustainably and "failing to act with the urgency necessary to tackle the plastic pollution crisis." For others, any company that feeds the consumer economy on the scale that Walmart does could never be green, no matter what else it does to mitigate the mess it has helped to create. Walmart's efforts "cannot be dismissed as greenwashing," said Stacy Mitchell of the Institute for Local Self-Reliance. "It's actually far more dangerous than that. Walmart's initiatives have just enough meat to have distracted much of the environmental movement, along with most journalists and many ordinary people, from the fundamental fact that, as a system of distributing goods to people, big-box retailing is as intrinsically unsustainable as clear-cut logging is as a method of harvesting trees."

But the naysayers notwithstanding, Walmart has come to be widely regarded as a corporate environmental leader—imperfect, yes, but a company that has taken the issues seriously and is making real progress in the right direction. What Walmart has done has been "objectively impressive," said Fred Krupp, the president of the Environmental Defense Fund, which in 2006 opened an office in Bentonville so his staff could advise the retailer even more closely. Elizabeth Sturcken, who leads the organization's partnerships with business, doesn't hesitate to say that Walmart still has plenty of shortcomings: setting strict enough production standards in China, impelling optimal fertilizer use among its suppliers, placing the bar as high as possible for its private-label brands, and more. But what it has done, including removing 20 million metric tons of greenhouse emissions from its supply chain and inducing the phase-out of eight hazardous chemicals found mostly in beauty and personal care items, has been extraordinary. "They are far from a sustainable company," Sturcken said. "But I do not believe that any other retailer has done more."

Walmart has also affected the larger landscape. Because of its size and stature, the company has caused ripples far beyond its own walls—just as Scott and Dach hoped it would. Thinking back to the early 2000s, when he was the head of Conservation International's Center for Environmental Leadership in Business, Glenn Prickett would realize that he was right at ground zero when corporate America began to look at environmental sustainability as integral to its own long-term profitability. No longer would it be seen merely as a compliance headache. In hindsight, Prickett would attribute this aha moment to three seminal developments: Hurricane Katrina, which prompted people to start focusing on the nexus between extreme weather and climate change; *An Inconvenient Truth*; and the greening of the biggest company in America. This awakening for business "traces directly back to the Walmart initiative," said Prickett, who participated in some of the first conversations with the retailer at Conservation International and would later become president of another nonprofit, the World Environment Center.

By the end of 2006, with Al Gore having barnstormed Bentonville and the Environmental Defense Fund having set up shop less than a mile from the Home Office, Walmart and the green movement no longer seemed like strange bedfellows; instead, they were now just bedfellows. In only a couple of months, however, the company would find itself part of a much odder pairing. Lee Scott and Andy Stern of the Service Employees

International Union were about to park themselves at a table and tell the press corps how, together, they intended to fix healthcare.

Normally, a news conference on Capitol Hill about expanding health coverage would not garner much attention, save for among the wonkiest of policy wonks and C-SPAN devotees. But there was nothing at all commonplace about having Lee Scott and Andy Stern—"two once-implacable foes," in the words of the *Washington Post*—come to the same dais in February 2007 to say that they were forming an alliance to help all Americans have access to quality and affordable medical insurance. It was "equivalent in my view to Anwar Sadat going to Jerusalem to shake hands with Menachem Begin," said Len Nichols, the director of health policy for the New America Foundation.

For Scott, liaising with the SEIU was another chance to show that Walmart was listening to its critics and becoming more socially responsible and, in this way, counter the opprobrium that continued to be directed at the company—including from the Walmart Watch campaign, which the union was still prosecuting even as Scott and Stern linked arms and called for "achieving a new American healthcare system by 2012." Without further repair to Walmart's reputation, Scott knew, the company might never overcome bitter opposition to building new stores in urban areas or appeal to more affluent shoppers, two ingredients that he thought vital to reversing the retailer's now-slowing sales growth. More to the point, healthcare inflation was crippling businesses of all kinds; at Walmart, it was rising about 20 percent a year. "We've all heard about the threat that soaring healthcare costs pose to the auto industry," Scott had told the National Governors Association in a February 2006 speech that caught Stern's attention. "But we'd be fooling ourselves to think any company in America is immune to those same pressures." Yet if health costs could somehow be contained and all frontline workers at an employer like Walmart could get the medical care they needed without it being a financial burden, it would bolster the economy and nullify a concern for which Scott's company had become the nation's poster child. "It makes a lot of business sense for them to try to get healthcare off the table," said Nelson Lichtenstein, the labor historian.

For Stern, finding a way for America's working families to get the healthcare they needed had become central to the SEIU's mission. It was a cause that transcended what the union itself could win during contract negotiations, much as Walter Reuther, the president of the United Auto Workers, had led the fight for national health insurance in the 1960s. Some of this was personal. In 2002, Stern's 13-year-old daughter, Cassie, had died after complications from spinal surgery. "If we had had a better healthcare system," Stern told friends, "Cassie might still be here with me." He was also pragmatic. "The employer-based system of health coverage is over," Stern had written the previous July in a *Wall Street Journal* op-ed. "This may sound shocking, coming from a union leader whose members bargain constantly with employers for healthcare benefits. But the system is collapsing, crushed by out-of-control costs, a revolutionary global economy, and masses of uninsured." It was time,

Stern said, for business leaders to join labor in overhauling the system. "I understand why CEOs are afraid of healthcare costs," he wrote in the *Journal*. "What I don't understand is why they are so timid about doing something about them."

Stern himself was as far from timid as you could get. After graduating from the University of Pennsylvania in 1972, he became a social worker in Philadelphia. One day, he saw a notice for a membership meeting at SEIU Local 668. "I went for the free pizza," he later said, "but stayed because I was fascinated with the work the labor representatives did, and how committed they were to changing lives." In 1977, at age 26, he became president of the local. And in 1984, he became organizing director for the whole union, helping the SEIU's membership to balloon while most of organized labor was withering. In 1996, Stern became president of the SEIU, and its heady growth continued. By the time he'd step down 14 years later, the union would have gone from 1.4 million members to a shade under two million, mostly by organizing "whole categories of workers that the rest of the labor movement was largely ignoring," columnist Harold Meyerson has written. These included janitors and caregivers—many of them immigrants, women, and people of color.

Not unlike Lee Scott, Stern had the courage to trade ideas with others, even those with whom he didn't see eye to eye on everything or even most things, whether it was Republican Newt Gingrich, the former Speaker of the House, or the president of the US Chamber of Commerce. He also cut deals with executives from nursing homes and hospitals that disquieted other unionists who were accustomed to being more adversarial. "The question is: How do you have a relationship among people who do have different interests?" Stern said. "Unions represent an interest. Employers represent a different interest. But it doesn't mean you can't find common ground and common interests. So I don't think we should approach employers as if they are the enemy." If he thought that it might help working people build a stable, middle-class life, Stern was more than willing to innovate and try something new. And if others didn't like his maverick ways, Stern professed not to care. "My daughter's death was one of those life-changing things where you say, 'All right, nothing can hurt me more than I've been hurt, so go for it.'"

It's a good thing his skin was thick. Despite all his success—or maybe because of it—Stern rankled many. Inside the SEIU, there were those who saw him as heavy-handed, dictatorial, and willing to enlarge the membership at all costs, even if it meant sacrificing the union's progressive ideals. Outside, he was polarizing. In 2005, the SEIU split off from the AFL-CIO, and Stern formed Change to Win, an upstart federation of seven unions that sought to halt labor's decades-long slide through more aggressive organizing. "Those who left the house of labor are weakening our house, and shame on them," said the head of the United Steelworkers. Others felt that Stern was arrogant and much too quick to cozy up to business, an impression that was only amplified after he united with Walmart on healthcare. "My union never got over it," said Joe Hansen of the UFCW, which was also part of Change to Win. "They viewed Andy as the devil."

Hansen was blindsided by Stern's appearance with Scott, hearing about it only a couple of hours before it started. "I was really pissed," he said. Wake Up Walmart then held its own press conference, dissing Stern for providing the retailer with a venue where it could look like it was doing something virtuous on healthcare. "Why anybody would decide to give a disingenuous player that stage is unconscionable," said the campaign's director, Paul Blank. In May, when Stern and Scott came together again for a healthcare presentation at a Hilton hotel in New York, Stern found himself where no union leader wants to be: dodging several hundred UFCW members protesting outside.

Hooking up with Walmart also put Stern out of step with others with whom he ordinarily would have been aligned: Democratic politicians jockeying for a run at the White House in 2008. The same month that Stern and Scott were meeting in New York, Senator Barack Obama was at a union forum in New Jersey where he was asked about his "intentions" regarding Walmart. "Well," he replied, "I know I won't shop there." The audience erupted into applause. It wasn't the first time Obama had taken a jab at the company. Six months earlier, during a conference call with Wake Up Walmart, he had said that the retailer was "in a position to do better by its workers," adding that there was a "moral responsibility to stand up and fight" for higher wages and ample health and retirement benefits. Not to be outdone, John Edwards and Hillary Clinton were hard on Walmart, as well—though in the case of Clinton, the finger-wagging was complicated. From 1986 to 1992, while she was First Lady of Arkansas and a prominent attorney in Little Rock, she had been a member of Walmart's board of directors. Now, she was pushing the company away as fast as possible. "Walmart's policies," Clinton said on the campaign trail, "do not reflect the best way of doing business and the values that I think are important in America."

The relationship between the SEIU and Walmart had been kindled in January 2006 during a secret meeting in Chicago. Jose Villarreal, a Walmart board member, had arranged the rendezvous at the request of Andy Stern's chief of staff, Kirk Adams, who knew Villarreal from Texas politics. (Adams's mother-in-law was the former governor, Ann Richards.) Like Leslie Dach, Villarreal was a Democratic Party stalwart who'd found his way into the Walmart fold. He'd grown up in a Mexican American enclave in East Chicago, Indiana, as one of 10 children stuffed into a two-bedroom apartment on the shores of Lake Michigan. "Talk about poverty," he said. His dad was a furnace operator at Inland Steel. Villarreal worked there too for a time and carried a union card from United Steelworkers Local 1010. After getting a law degree, he became a civil rights lawyer, litigating fair housing and municipal services discrimination cases in East Texas. He later went to work for the Southwest Voter Registration and Education Project and then joined the Texas Attorney General's Office. Eventually, he became a partner at a big white-shoe firm in San Antonio, Akin Gump Strauss Hauer & Feld. He was also active in presidential politics, becoming deputy manager of the Clinton-Gore campaign in 1992.

In 1998, Villarreal was asked to join the board at Walmart. "They were really curious about the growing Hispanic market," he said. "They asked very incisive questions about the Latino community." The company also appreciated that his political connections on the left could be helpful. "They were just then beginning to feel organized pressure," said Villarreal, who was on the board of the US Congressional Hispanic Caucus Institute and the National Council of La Raza, a leading civil rights organization. Although Villarreal had come of age "under the romanticism of Cesar Chavez, the United Farm Workers movement, and all of that," he said, he didn't have "a strict ideological bent." Mainly, "it was such an honor for somebody of my background to be invited to serve on the board of the largest company and employer in the country."

Not every moment was gratifying. Villarreal was there, right in the front row, the day that John Tate called labor unions "blood-sucking parasites." "I just sank in my seat," Villarreal said. Yet the more he visited stores and talked with frontline employees, the more he came to believe that they were being treated well. "Some may find the rhetoric corny, but it was real at Walmart about respect for the individual," he said. "Sure, you had people who were unhappy. But by and large, the workforce at Walmart, at least from my experience, was very, very proud of the company." This perception made it all the more difficult for Villarreal to see Walmart "being crucified" by the SEIU and UFCW. "It was very painful for all of us—for me, especially," he said. "You know, these are a lot of my friends out there who were beating the hell out of us."

After the SEIU asked for a meeting, Villarreal contacted someone he thought would be the ideal facilitator: Henry Cisneros, the former mayor of San Antonio who'd been secretary of Housing and Urban Development during the Clinton administration. Cisneros knew both sides well. As a cabinet member, he'd met Andy Stern, and their friendship blossomed when the two later served together on the board of a philanthropy, the Broad Foundations. In the meantime, after he left office, Cisneros had become president of Univision, the Spanish-language television network. Walmart was a big advertiser, and Cisneros had gone to Bentonville, where he'd been enthralled by Sam Walton's old storefront on the town square. "It may be my weakness," Cisneros said, "but I love stories of people and their origins." Earlier, as mayor of San Antonio during the 1980s, "I saw families who had products that they otherwise could not have owned, from television sets to furniture to children's clothing, were it not for Walmart prices," Cisneros added. He wasn't blind to the company's problems, including the paltry wages it paid. But "I like creating solutions, not demonizing," Cisneros said—and so he was more than happy to play a part in getting the company and the union in the same room.

Walmart was represented by Villarreal and Tom Hyde, a corporate executive vice president. Stern, Adams, and two other top union officials, Judy Scott and Eliseo Medina, made up the SEIU contingent. "It had elements of cloak-and-dagger to it because they were all so nervous," Cisneros said. "It was, 'Did anybody see us coming in? We're going to go down by a back elevator.'" Once they laid eyes on each other, it was a typical first date—a bit awkward, with both parties trying to figure out where all of this might lead, yet without wanting to seem too forward.

As the others listened in, Stern and Hyde ruminated over whether any big organization, be it a union or a company, could ever really stay on top of things in the trenches or whether, said Hyde, "we were just kind of banging our way through this without fully understanding what the concerns of our respective employees and members were." Hyde was surprised that Stern was so open with him, and he was surprised at himself for responding in kind. "It just never entered my mind that you'd have that sort of conversation with somebody from a union," said Hyde, who before coming to Walmart had been the general counsel of Raytheon, the aerospace company. "I'd always assumed that they're going to be pretty guarded, and we're going to be pretty guarded."

As everyone got up to leave, Cisneros held back, lingering with Stern. He felt he had to tell him what he'd been agonizing about—if word ever got out that the SEIU leader was having a back-channel parley with Walmart, he might be physically harmed by someone in the labor movement who would see it as the ultimate betrayal.

"I worry about you as a friend," Cisneros told Stern. "I worry about your safety."

Nothing concrete was decided that day, but the union and the company agreed to keep talking. "Eye-awakening/unclear its implications," Judy Scott, the SEIU's top lawyer, wrote in her notes after the meeting. Eight weeks later, Stern and Walmart's Lee Scott came face-to-face for the first time. Bill Clinton, who'd been made aware of Stern's wish to meet the CEO, had asked both men to his suite at the MGM Grand in Las Vegas. Stern was in town for a Change to Win convention, and Scott was in Vegas on business. Clinton was raising money for his wife's 2006 Senate campaign. The encounter was brief, but Stern was able to build on the groundwork laid at the Chicago meeting. "I'm not here to make trouble," he told Scott. "I think there are areas like healthcare we could really do some work on."

In the months that followed, the SEIU and Walmart met about a half-dozen times, including in Bentonville—all of it kept tightly under wraps. Tom Hyde was the point person for the company, and he quickly earned the trust of those from the

SEIU. "He was a very honorable guy," Adams said. Unlike many Walmart executives, Hyde was not reflexively anti-union. As a young man, in between the Army and law school, he'd worked at the Missouri Pacific Railroad, where he joined the Brotherhood of Railway and Steamship Clerks, Freight Handlers, Express, and Station Employees. It was then that he saw the good that could come from constructive give-and-take between labor and management. "I would have been an officer in that union had I decided to stay on as a railroad worker," Hyde said. As the talks with the SEIU gained steam, "we went down three roads," Adams said: healthcare reform, worker voice, and wages.

On healthcare, there was a sense from the outset that, at least in broad strokes, Walmart and the union could find some consensus. "We had a lot of overlap on what we thought the issues were," said Linda Dillman, a Walmart executive vice president who managed the company's medical benefits. "We may not have agreed completely on who should play what role in healthcare. But we agreed in terms of what direction we thought the country should go."

Dillman came to this realization during a meeting with Gina Glantz, a senior adviser to Andy Stern who had come to Bentonville to see her. "There was no way we were going to march somebody from the SEIU into the Home Office," Dillman said, and so they wound up at Dillman's house. The setting lent itself to a level of intimacy that might otherwise have been absent—two women talking not just about health policy but about their families and their lives. "When you oppose someone and that's your job, you have to work up a certain edge about them to go after them in the way you do," said Glantz, who had run Bill Bradley's presidential campaign before coming to the SEIU. "And then you meet them and they're human and they have human stories, as she did." Dillman was disarmed, as well. "It is interesting when you actually sit down with people that you think are your enemy," she said, "and you find out they're just another human being, dealing with the same things you are."

On the subject of worker voice, the idea was to set up some kind of telephone hotline, monitored by the union, so that if a toxic store manager was, say, forcing hourly employees to work off the clock or sexually harassing them, they had a place to report the misconduct where they knew they'd be protected. For those who didn't feel comfortable using Mr. Sam's open-door policy, this would be a secure alternative. And it could help tip off Walmart to the types of problems that were costing it dearly both in legal settlements and bad publicity. The notion was that "people will be more likely to talk to us," Stern said. "We could function as sort of an ombudsperson." The SEIU and Walmart also kicked around a variation of the concept in which there would be a store-level "compliance code that we could all sign off on" and that would include "worker involvement and enforcement," Adams said.

On wages, the discussion revolved around whether Walmart would agree in the urban areas it was trying to enter to pay its workers a prevailing amount that wouldn't undercut what the UFCW had negotiated with other supermarkets in those cities. In return, the unions wouldn't oppose Walmart's move into these locations.

As the SEIU and Walmart continued to meet through 2006, Stern kept Joe Hansen apprised. The UFCW leader knew his union was in no position to sit down alone with Walmart, but he also knew that the SEIU—because it wasn't trying to get to a collective bargaining agreement with the company—might be able to hash out some things and, ultimately, even bring the UFCW into the deliberations. "It's kind of like Switzerland has to carry on the conversation in certain situations," Stern said.

In actuality, the SEIU was equal parts noncombatant and combatant. As the union and Walmart met surreptitiously, Walmart Watch kept hammering away—a course that might sound schizophrenic but was actually strategic. Although those on the Walmart Watch campaign were not privy to the particulars of what Stern and the other higher-ups at the SEIU were mulling with the company, they knew that something was afoot, and by maintaining pressure, they hoped to help pave a way forward. "Our job was to bang on the door, and Andy Stern's job was to walk through it," said David Nassar, who'd replaced Andy Grossman as Walmart Watch's executive director.

As Stern and Scott finally came out under the flag "Better Health Care Together," they were criticized for being long on generalities—"Employers, individuals, and public sources like Medicaid and Medicare need to appropriately share costs," they said—and short on details. "People at the Brookings Institution joke, 'Next month we're going to have four different proposals about universal healthcare, and Andy Stern's going to be supporting all four,'" Stern admitted.

But over time, Walmart and the SEIU would throw their combined weight behind a very specific provision that would help lead to tens of millions of Americans becoming insured. In the summer of 2009, with Barack Obama now in the Oval Office, the company, the union, and the left-leaning Center for American Progress came out in favor of a cornerstone of the administration's healthcare plan: a requirement for employers to provide medical coverage to their workers or help pay for it. Walmart was among the only large companies to endorse an employer mandate. Leslie Dach delivered the joint letter to the White House. The National Retail Federation said it was "flabbergasted." The *Wall Street Journal* editorial page knocked Walmart for "selling out its competitors."

By this time, both Walmart Watch and Wake Up Walmart had mostly faded away. "You can't keep up that white hot level of energy," said Meghan Scott, the deputy director of Wake Up Walmart. Others who had led the group, including Paul Blank and Buffy Wicks, had departed in 2007 to work on different presidential campaigns. Walmart had also taken some heat off itself by offering less expensive health insurance, resulting in higher enrollment by its hourly employees. The upshot, the *New York Times* said, was that "it is now easier for many to sign up for healthcare at Walmart than at its rival Target." Considering this, it was harder than before to make Walmart the bogeyman. On top of that, said Nassar of Walmart Watch, "a certain amount of fatigue about writing the Walmart-is-bad story" had set in for the media.

In early 2009, Walmart had gotten a new CEO: Mike Duke, who'd headed the company's international operations before taking over for Lee Scott. As Scott retired, the Environmental Defense Fund's Fred Krupp had only kind words for him. "I almost think of Lee Scott as a Gorbachev leading glasnost, because Lee was this figure that opened Walmart's walls up to the outside," he said. Indeed, Walmart had changed so much under Scott that it now found itself being attacked from a new direction: the right. In May 2009, the conservative National Legal and Policy Center said the company was "cowering to activist pressure" and "doing little to defend the free-market principles that have made it so successful."

But despite his own rapprochement with Scott, Andy Stern couldn't resist issuing a last shot: What "Lee Scott never really came . . . to appreciate is, the leader of the largest private-sector company in the world has an opportunity and an ability to set a different standard in the marketplace," Stern said. Instead, by keeping Walmart's workers at an average wage of $10.68 an hour, the departing CEO had watered down his own legacy. Choosing not to share more of the company's profits, said Stern, "is the missing link for Lee Scott's greatness."

There were moments when the SEIU had thought it might be on the cusp of a deal around a prevailing wage. "I can remember a couple of times coming home from these trips and feeling, 'Yeah, we might have something here,'" Adams said. But the colloquy petered out.

Walmart had come a long way on a host of issues, including the environment and universal healthcare. It had lobbied for an extension of the Voting Rights Act and, along with Reverend Al Sharpton, for passage of comprehensive immigration reform. But where it had the most direct control—deciding how much to pay its workers—it hadn't moved an inch. Six months before he gave his big speech following Hurricane Katrina, Lee Scott had given a sense of why. "Some well-meaning critics contend that Walmart should be setting the pace for wages and benefits for the entire economy, just as a unionized General Motors was said to have done in the postwar period, helping usher in the great American middle class that this country is so proud of," he said. "The facts are that retailing doesn't perform that same function in the economy as GM does or did. Retailing has never occupied the top tier of wages in this country, or in any country." Walmart never seemed to get beyond this view.

If anything, the company was going in the wrong direction on pay. In late 2010, Walmart said it would end profit sharing—the extra compensation that Sam Walton had called "the carrot that's kept Walmart headed forward." Instead of automatically placing up to 4 percent of a worker's earnings into a profit-sharing plan, the company would instead put up to 6 percent in a 401(k) retirement plan—but only as a match; the employee had to contribute first. Walmart said the switch would make its retirement benefits more "contemporary." But mostly, it was a way to cut expenses. "The beauty of this seemingly magnanimous offer is that many low-paid retail workers don't participate" in 401(k) plans because they don't make enough money to sock anything away, a columnist for CBS MoneyWatch wrote, adding that "given what Walmart pays," it's "unsurprising that…workers are pissed." Burt Flickinger III, a retail consultant, equated Walmart taking away profit sharing with Ebenezer Scrooge. "Ebenezer makes all the money," he said, "and all the poor Cratchits working in the Walmart stores become poorer and poorer."

Five years after Lee Scott had staked out "what leadership means for Walmart in the 21st century," the company had opened its ears to many of its critics. It had opened its mind to many new ideas. It had yet, however, to open its wallet to its own employees.

CHAPTER 4

Occupy Walmart

AS HUNDREDS OF people descended upon New York City's Zuccotti Park in the fall of 2011 under the rallying cry of Occupy Wall Street, not everyone was positive what the demonstrators were trying to achieve—not even the demonstrators themselves. The *Times* characterized the encampment of blue, red, and orange tents that had sprung up as "a diffuse and leaderless convocation of activists." They'd assembled, the paper said, "to air societal grievances as carnival," right down to the dissidents outfitted in mustachioed Guy Fawkes masks, a tribute to the insurrectionist who tried to bomb British Parliament in 1605. The *Washington Post* called it "a protest movement without clear demands." But on this October day, there was nothing amorphous about what one group who had come to the park was trying to accomplish: they wanted Walmart to raise workers' wages.

"We're here today to let the people at Occupy Wall Street know that Walmart's associates stand with them; we are the 99 percent," said Girshriela Green, who had gone to work at the company in 2009 as a part-timer in the Crenshaw neighborhood of Los Angeles. After several raises and a promotion to manager of the health and beauty department, she had seen her pay climb—but not by much. After starting at $8.20 an hour, Green had reached $9.80 before hurting her arm on the job, an injury that she blamed on having to manually haul 100 heavy boxes each day because of understaffing at her store. "For too long," Green said, "Walmart has pushed its associates around, and it's time we got the dignity and respect we deserve."

A Walmart spokesman said Green's comments were "particularly misguided given the fact that Walmart is focused on serving the 99 percent." Whatever the case, Walmart was now caught in an uncomfortable and all-too-familiar position: responding to bad press that had been orchestrated by the United Food and Commercial Workers.

Green was part of a new group, the Organization United for Respect at Walmart, or OUR Walmart, which the UFCW had launched the previous summer. It had been a few years since the union's Wake Up Walmart campaign went relatively silent. Yet "I never gave up on Walmart," said Pat O'Neill, who had become the UFCW's director of organizing during that quiescent phase. "I knew we had to do something." Officially, under the constraints of labor law, OUR Walmart wasn't supposed to try to become the bargaining agent for workers or even serve as a vehicle for the UFCW to do so. But, not unlike with Wake Up

Walmart, the union always hoped that the renewed vexing might turn into a successful bank shot, bringing the company to the negotiating table indirectly and leading to a contract. "I knew how hard it was going to be," O'Neill said. "I just think that's what you have to do. It's like if you're a priest, you've got to keep out there until you've saved the flock."

What was different this time was OUR Walmart's center of gravity. The UFCW knew it didn't stand a chance of getting anywhere with a traditional collective bargaining campaign; the company had long ago shown that it was impervious to such efforts. And using political operatives to inflame the public about Walmart had also run its course. To chart a new path, the UFCW invited an eclectic group to Washington: labor and community organizers alongside experts on antitrust and supply-chain issues. "It was like a mini Manhattan Project," said Dan Schlademan, who, after helping to lead the Service Employees International Union's Justice for Janitors campaign, had been hired by the UFCW in early 2010 to formulate a fresh approach for taking on Walmart. "We locked people into a conference space for a bunch of days, and we tore apart a ton of information, a ton of history. When the meeting was over, there was a lot of cohesion around that we were never going to do this from the outside in. This needs to be worker-led."

Hourly employees had been involved here and there in Wake Up Walmart and Walmart Watch, but never to the extent Schlademan was envisaging. Even the name—OUR Walmart—"was a perspective shift," said Jason Young, a Washington consultant with ASGK Public Strategies, which the UFCW had engaged to sharpen its plans. The notion was to frame the needs of Walmart associates "from the associates' perspective, not from the union's perspective, and not from any other perspective." As ASGK elaborated in an early presentation to the union: the "our" in OUR Walmart "represents the age-old idea that the most important stakeholders in the workplace are the workers themselves....It conveys ownership in the company where associates already work—the kind of ownership that comes from banding together in a unified voice."

The concept wasn't entirely novel. At an earlier point, the UFCW had briefly experimented with a similar group known as Walmart Workers of America. And in 2005, in league with the UFCW, Wade Rathke of the SEIU had signed up about 1,000 hourly employees in Florida as dues-paying members of the Walmart Workers Association. The intention was for them to "push and shove" from inside the company for increased compensation and better conditions without going through the arduous exercise of gaining union representation and winning a formal contract. "We are building something that's never been seen," Rathke said at the time. "It's neither fish nor fowl." Despite the traction that Rathke and his organizers were able to get with workers in more than 30 stores, top union officials weren't interested then in replicating what he'd done, and the template fizzled.

Now, though, the UFCW was all in. "We've fought in every way we know how" against Walmart, said Joe Hansen, the union's president. The time had come "to connect more directly with the workers in the store." Still, figuring out how OUR Walmart should go about this wasn't so simple. As ASGK did its research, it realized that while a worker-centric group was the way to go, not every hourly employee at Walmart was ripe for membership. The firm divided people into five groups, zero through four. Ones were those rare Walmart workers who had signed a union card. Twos were pro-union but hadn't yet signed. Threes were more neutral—neither pro-union nor anti-union. Fours were anti-union. And zeroes were "anti-Walmart."

The twos and threes were the sweet spot. Anyone who was overtly anti-union was likely to be a bad fit for OUR Walmart. But so were the zeros. They were so resentful of the company that they already had one foot out the door. "How do you organize somebody who's going to be gone in three months?" Young asked. "That made no sense to my brain. We needed the people who were going to stay there either because they loved the place and wanted to make it better or because they had no other choice. Those were the people who were going to stick around and make a difference." Among these twos and threes, Young added, "we were trying to create a sense of community. We were creating space for these associates to talk to each other about what their experiences were and what they wanted—what their vision was."

Schlademan's beachhead was a Walmart in Laurel, Maryland. This was, in large part, because the store was home to Cindy Murray, who had been working there in the fitting room since 2000. Murray wasn't completely "anti-Walmart"—a zero on the ASGK scale. Although she was making less than $20,000 a year, there were things about her job that she truly enjoyed, especially the companionship. "People at Walmart stay at Walmart because of the people," she said. "They stay there because of the other workers. And not just that. You build a relationship with certain customers that come all the time." But Murray also recognized Walmart's defects, which she thought had gotten worse over the previous five years, at least at her store. As she saw it, the bosses in Bentonville were leaning on her local managers to cut costs even more than before, and that was taking a toll on her and other hourly employees, who were being praised less and oppressed more. While "the pay always sucked," said Murray, "we had fun." Then, all of a sudden, she said, "you could see a quick decline in the way they treated the workers."

Along with acknowledging both good and bad in the company (emphasis on the bad), Murray had another attribute that made her the perfect founding member of OUR Walmart: she was brave. In 2006, after a run-in with a supervisor, Murray had contacted the UFCW about organizing her store, and she had been a vocal presence ever since, appearing at union rallies, taking part in a Wake Up Walmart television ad, and testifying before the Maryland legislature to call upon the company to improve its health coverage. "If we become silent," Murray asked, "then what happens?"

Schlademan estimated that somewhere between 10 and 30 percent of the workers at every single Walmart across the country were "courageous people like Cindy, who are ready to do what it's going to take" to fight for change from within. "And when you do that horizontally" across hundreds, if not thousands, of stores, he said, "that's a powerful group." To make itself even more potent, OUR Walmart allied with Warehouse Workers United, which was seeking to recover back pay for those who claimed they'd been cheated while loading and unloading Walmart products at a giant distribution complex outside Los Angeles.

As the leaders and most visible members of OUR Walmart emerged, it was apparent that most of these hourly employees had something else in common besides their pluck: they were women—Ernestine Bassett, who worked at the same Walmart as Cindy Murray in Maryland; Girshriela Green, Maggie Van Ness, Evelin Cruz, Denise Barlage, and Venanzi Luna in California; Mary Pat Tifft in Wisconsin; Angela Williamson, Wessa Milien, and Gloria Taylor in Florida; Janet Sparks in Louisiana; Patricia Scott in Washington. This wasn't surprising. In step with societal norms, Sam Walton had inveterately put young men into management roles and funneled women into low-paying frontline jobs. Through the 1970s, "each company newsletter showcased an endlessly repeated vignette: store managers in their 20s"—all of them male—"presenting five- and ten-year service pins to women who could be their mothers or even grandmothers," Columbia University historian Bethany Moreton has noted. "Like much of the service sector that waxed as manufacturing waned, Walmart and retail generally" had come to rely on "categories of employees it could imagine as less than breadwinners," including wives and mothers. As the decades went by, the picture wasn't quite as sexist, but the underlying pattern remained intact: at the moment Cindy Murray and other early OUR Walmart members began to mobilize, women made up about 57 percent of the company's workforce, but they accounted for nearly 72 percent of its sales associates and only 41 percent of its managers and corporate executives.

From the beginning, OUR Walmart sought to galvanize around the energy and passion—and pique—of Walmart's frontline employees. "The first thing we did was a deep, deep listening process with thousands of people who worked at Walmart to identify what are the things that they really wanted and needed," said Andrea Dehlendorf, another Justice for

Janitors alum who joined Schlademan in early 2011 to help oversee OUR Walmart. That June, OUR Walmart went live with a Facebook page as the centerpiece of its recruitment drive. The organization hoped to draw people there through ads aimed at the 150,000 people whose profiles on the social network revealed that they were Walmart employees. Once they hit the site, they were to be greeted by a string of posts—some of them, ASGK recommended, "hopeful, positive, humorous" and others "negative, righteous, or even angry"—that would inspire them to comment or, better yet, become an OUR Walmart member for $5 a month in dues. "Our schedules are often irregular and inflexible, making it difficult to care for our families," read one early post. "Walmart should make scheduling more predictable and dependable. If you agree with this statement and other ways OUR Walmart is suggesting Walmart improve, sign on...below."

Within two weeks, according to the UFCW, some 65,000 people had visited OUR Walmart's Facebook page, and workers from several dozen stores were joining up. At some locations, the group would soon claim 50 or more members. "Someone has to stand up to say something," said Deondra Thomas, who was making $8.90 an hour in the shoe department of a Walmart in Dallas after three years there. "So many people have been quiet for so long. A lot of us think Walmart is an awesome company, but as far as the employees, they treat us like dirt."

On June 15, 97 OUR Walmart members headed to Bentonville for the organization's coming-out party. Together, they drew up a "Declaration of Respect" with a preamble that communicated feelings of both dignity and indignation: "We, the hourly associates, are the lifeblood of Walmart. Our company is stronger because of the values we embrace—a strong work ethic, compassion for one another, and honesty. Yet we are not treated with the respect we deserve."

Their 12-point manifesto, which recalled Sam Walton's promise of "respect for the individual," asserted that the company should pay everyone at least $13 an hour and increase the percentage of full-time workers; make scheduling "more predictable and dependable"; offer genuinely affordable health coverage; fix the open-door policy for workers with complaints since those trying to use it "have found that their issues are not resolved and confidentiality is not respected"; end "retaliation" against those who are "speaking out about issues at work"; have a liaison at corporate headquarters who, in the case of someone being fired, would hear out the employee; put in place "affirmative policies that secure full access to opportunity and equal treatment to all associates regardless of gender identity, race, disability, sexual orientation, or age"; and follow through in several other areas. Walking the line between confrontation and cooperation, the declaration ended this way: "We envision a world where we succeed in our careers, our company succeeds in business, our customers receive great service and value, and Walmart and associates share all of these goals."

On June 16, the OUR Walmart members gathered at the Home Office to hand-deliver the declaration to company officials. They were met outside the front doors by Karen Casey, Walmart's senior vice president for labor relations.

"Nice to meet you," Casey said as she shook hands with Sarita Gupta, the executive director of Jobs With Justice, a workers' rights advocacy organization, who had accompanied the OUR Walmart brigade. "Welcome to Bentonville. Nice to see you."

"The intention with which everyone is here is really to open up dialogue because we all want to make the best Walmart possible," Gupta told Casey.

Surrounded by workers clad in lime green OUR Walmart T-shirts, Casey assured the group that "our cornerstone at Walmart is around respect for the individual, and we expect that to be exercised."

Misty Tanner, an OUR Walmart member from Richmond, California, was having none of it. "Well, that needs to drain down to the stores," she said, cutting Casey off. "You guys clone your management to disrespect these associates. It's the associates that do the backbreaking work that make you guys your pennies every day."

When Casey vowed that "we do not tolerate any type of retaliation" against employees who bring up concerns, she was met by a chorus of disbelief. "That's the policy," one worker said, "but that's not what happens."

"We need to know the individual circumstances so that we can do right by each associate," Casey said.

"I think the key thing here as we talk," Gupta replied, "is these aren't individual situations. It's actually a problem throughout the company."

Casey explained that Walmart regularly administered a pulse survey to its 1.4 million US employees, implying that the company was on top of anything that might be causing widespread dissatisfaction. "We take those results to heart to try to make sure that our policies work," she said.

But Tanner, a former assistant manager herself, questioned the integrity of the survey. "We were directed by our store manager to stand behind our associates to make sure they weren't...putting down the wrong thing to make our store manager look bad," she told Casey. "I was told to stand behind my overnighters—Jerry was one of them—to make sure he wasn't putting in the wrong answers," she continued, gesturing to a worker in the crowd. She then pointed to Kim, another employee from Richmond, and said she monitored her answers too.

"I am sorry about the situation you just relayed in your store," Casey said.

"It's not just my store," said Tanner, prompting the chorus to start up again: "It's nationwide!" several people yelled.

"I'm really here to listen," Casey said. "I'm not meaning to diminish anything that you're saying. Certainly, we want to take these issues to heart to make this a better Walmart."

As the confab ended, one of Casey's colleagues stepped in. "We'll take this," she said as Casey held up a poster-sized version of the OUR Walmart declaration. "We'll share it with our senior management. We'll go through the individual points. You guys have made a great emotional case. So let us take it seriously and see what we can do."

This would mark the last time that Walmart and OUR Walmart would ever have this kind of exchange. In the period to come, each side would become more truculent. Any real conversation was done.

On June 20, just four days after members of OUR Walmart had congregated in front of the Home Office, the US Supreme Court issued a much-anticipated decision in the giant gender bias case against Walmart that had been percolating since before Lee Scott's post-Katrina speech. The suit was originated by Betty Dukes, a 54-year-old worker at a Walmart in Pittsburg, California, where she had started in 1994 as a part-time cashier.

In many ways, her experience mirrored what the delegation from OUR Walmart had been describing to Karen Casey. Dukes had a real fondness for her job, having grown close with other employees and many of her store's shoppers. "It was her family away from her family," her niece Rita Roland said. But she was also fed up. After she was promoted a couple of times and became an hourly customer service manager, Dukes asked to receive training so she could advance even further. Instead, she watched those opportunities go to male employees who were newer to Walmart. When she complained, she started to be written up for trifling offenses, such as returning from break a bit late—an infraction that others in the store committed all the time without any consequences. Eventually, Dukes was demoted and had her pay cut.

"I felt that I was victimized," she said, adding that "I started up the chain of command with upper management to no avail." In June 2001, having come to understand that what happened to her was far from unique, Dukes became the lead plaintiff in a lawsuit alleging that the retailer had discriminated against women in its pay, benefits, and promotions. At her church, Dukes tried to tell her friends about what she was doing in a way they could relate to: "*Betty Dukes v. Walmart* is like David versus Goliath," she would say.

But on this day, Goliath dropped David. Voting 5–4 along ideological lines, the Supreme Court found that the lawsuit filed on behalf of 1.6 million women failed to meet the requirement that "there are questions of law or fact common to the class" of female employees at the company. Rather, Justice Antonin Scalia wrote in his opinion, the plaintiffs were trying to bring a suit "about literally millions of employment decisions at once" without "some glue holding the alleged reasons for all those decisions together."

By narrowing what constituted a class action, and thereby limiting the ability of others to join together in such a suit, the justices handed not just Walmart but all of corporate America an enormous victory. Robin Conrad, an attorney for the US Chamber of Commerce, called it "the most important class-action case in more than a decade." Suzette Malveaux, a professor at the University of Colorado Law School, said the ruling had "tipped the balance in favor of powerful employers over everyday workers." Had Walmart lost, it could have owed the women billions of dollars in damages.

Naturally, the retailer praised the high court's decision, which reversed a lower-court ruling. "As the majority made clear, the plaintiffs' claims were worlds away from showing a company-wide discriminatory pay and promotion policy," it said in a statement. Gisel Ruiz, a Walmart executive vice president, maintained that the outcome of the case "pulls the rug out from under the accusations made against Walmart over the last 10 years."

Nevertheless, for the company, considerable harm to its reputation had already been done. Even though the court found that the plaintiffs hadn't come close to proving that Walmart "operated under a general policy of discrimination," their legal team had introduced a statistical analysis indicating that female employees at the company made 5 to 15 percent less than men in equivalent roles, even though women on average had higher performance ratings and more years on the job. And while the court said that the 120 affidavits filed in the case were too weak to warrant a class action, these sworn statements did Walmart no favors in its bid to come across as a more socially responsible employer. One male supervisor had allegedly said that "women weren't qualified to be managers because men had an extra rib." Another reportedly remarked that the role of a female assistant manager was to give women workers someone to talk about their periods with. Female employees said they were called "Janie Qs" and "squatters," a reference to how they peed. One female worker said she was told that "men need to be paid more because they have families to support." Others said they heard the same sort of rationalization for why their wages were so low.

Sue Oliver, a seasoned human resources executive brought in from American Airlines by Lee Scott to help shore up many of Walmart's HR practices, said that when she arrived in 2004, there were "a few bad apples" among the company's store managers. Their "general misconduct," she said, "had been, perhaps, tolerated in the past"—vestiges of a Southern retailer that, in hardly any time at all, had become America's largest corporation. But Oliver said that Scott and Mike Duke, who led Walmart's US operations at that time, fully backed her as she revised all sorts of protocols, including moving scores of newly hired HR professionals into the field across the country; before, a much smaller HR staff had been centralized in Bentonville. Both Scott and Duke, she said, were insistent that the "kind of culture that has somehow grown up is no longer us. We don't want that to be us." And in short order, Oliver said, the "good old boys' network got broken up." Once store managers had "the support they needed to make good, fair decisions with their teams," she added, "we actually faced little resistance" to abiding by the rules.

Ever since Scott had called on Walmart to be "at our best, all the time," this had become a familiar refrain: we may have made some serious mistakes in the past, but that's not who we are now.

OUR Walmart, however, contended that the company wasn't nearly as evolved as its top executives believed it to be. Soon after the Supreme Court ruled in the *Dukes* case, the group released a poll of some 500 Walmart workers, which showed that women fared worse at the company than men when it came to pay, respect, retirement benefits, training for promotions, job security, and fair procedures for disciplining, firing, or laying off workers. "It's not that working at Walmart is a wonderful experience for men," said Celinda Lake, who conducted the poll. "It's just that Walmart is especially tough on women."

It wouldn't be the last time that OUR Walmart used a major event in the news as a springboard to attack the company. In April 2012, as Walmart became engulfed in a bribery scandal at its Mexican subsidiary, OUR Walmart leader Venanzi Luna started an online petition calling for Mike Duke to step down as CEO and Rob Walton to resign as chairman. "Nobody should get away with bribery, and they should be held accountable for that," said Luna, who worked in the deli at the Walmart in Pico Rivera, California.

Mostly, though, OUR Walmart made its own news. In early October, for the first time in Walmart's history, workers at multiple stores went out on strike against the company. "Who's got the power?" they shouted. "We've got the power! What kind of power? People power!" The one-day walkout by 60 or so hourly employees at nine Walmarts around Los Angeles was more symbolic than substantive; all the stores were able to open for business without a hitch. But as they rallied, the workers put the spotlight on an issue that, in their view, was becoming increasingly alarming: although Karen Casey had assured OUR Walmart that its members would not face any reprisal for sounding off, the group said that several of its leaders had been disciplined or fired since the 2011 trip to Bentonville. "Anyone who goes against management, you're pretty much putting a target on your back," said Monique Velasquez, a striking employee in Pico Rivera, which had become the center of OUR Walmart activity. "They intimidate you by cutting hours or picking on you in any way they can." Walmart denied that this was the case.

The Southern California walkout was just a warm-up. Strikes spread from there to a dozen other cities. And in November, OUR Walmart members across the United States led a series of walkouts on the biggest shopping day of the year—Black Friday, the day after Thanksgiving. It was a protest, the organization said, against the company's "attempts to silence associates who have spoken out against things like Walmart's low take-home pay, unpredictable work schedules, unaffordable health benefits," and more.

The actions did little, if anything, to cut into the retailer's sales. Although OUR Walmart coordinated more than 1,000 demonstrations around the country, often in partnership with local community activists, only about 100 Walmart employees actually walked off the job—a mere 0.007 percent of the company's US workforce. Even calling that a blip would be an overstatement. Walmart, meanwhile, said that it enjoyed its best Black Friday ever, with customers across the nation scooping up nearly 5,000 items per second from 8 p.m. to midnight—the height of the hunt for a good deal. "Walmart Strike Proves to

Be a Turkey," read a headline in *Chain Store Age*, a trade publication.

But if the walkouts didn't sabotage the company's business, they did sabotage the image that Walmart was trying so hard to project. Coverage of the strikes was way out of proportion to the number of workers participating, with many column inches devoted to frontline employees talking about how crummy their jobs were. On the NBC Nightly News, the phrase "Taking a Stand" appeared on the screen over anchor Brian Williams's shoulder. OUR Walmart couldn't have staged it any better. "The totality of it was really a media tsunami," said Eddie Iny, OUR Walmart's campaigns director.

Tyrone Robinson, who earned $8.95 an hour in the produce department of a Supercenter in Chicago, said he was protesting because his store had started to use more temp workers to save on costs. That led to a reduction in his hours, forcing him to give up his apartment and move in with an aunt. "I just can't be silent no more," Robinson told a reporter. Sara Gilbert, a customer service manager in Seattle, said her hourly wage came out to just $14,000 a year. "I work full-time for one of the richest companies in the world," she said, "and my kids get state health insurance and are on food stamps." Colby Harris, who made $8.90 an hour after working for three years at a Walmart in Lancaster, Texas, spoke of needing a "buddy system" to scrape by. "We loan each other money during non-paycheck weeks just to make it through to the next week when we get paid because we don't have enough money...to even eat lunch," he said. He also bristled at the complaint the company had filed with federal regulators arguing that OUR Walmart was perpetrating unfair labor practices. "Unfair labor," Harris said, "is working full-time and living in poverty."

Publicly, Walmart did its best to minimize the significance of the strikes. A corporate spokesman called them "just another exaggerated publicity campaign aimed at generating headlines to mislead." But inside the company, OUR Walmart's combination of audacity and efficacy wasn't lost on anyone. "It absolutely shook them up," said Dehlendorf, whose picture was posted in various stores, the way a bank robber's photo gets tacked up near the teller's window, so that managers could immediately recognize her and alert security if she walked in.

As *Bloomberg Businessweek* would lay out, after digesting more than 1,000 pages of internal documents, the company considered OUR Walmart "enough of a threat that it hired an intelligence-gathering service from Lockheed Martin, contacted the FBI, staffed up its labor hotline, ranked stores by labor activity, and kept eyes on employees (and activists) prominent in the group." Employees "across the company were watched; the briefest conversations were reported" to the Home Office.

Walmart also tried to wrest control of the narrative. In May 2013, the retailer began airing national television ads called "The Real Walmart." One explored how the company used its mastery of purchasing and logistics to deliver low prices. Another featured happy customers who benefited from all the money they'd saved by shopping at Walmart, whether it was to help pay for a kid's braces or squirrel away a little extra dough for college. In a third set of commercials, a Walmart truck driver, a onetime intern who rose up to be a store manager, and a 19-year-old hourly worker looking forward to building a career at the company all spoke glowingly of their jobs.

These weren't outliers. A survey conducted in October 2012 by Walmart found that 87 percent of full-timers and 85 percent of part-timers "really love" their job, while 88 percent of the former and 91 percent of the latter "would definitely recommend" the company to a friend seeking employment.

In their analysis—based on more than 600,000 posts to an employee discussion board, 9,000-plus evaluations of the company on the job-review site Glassdoor, 6,000 responses from Walmart workers to an online survey, and more than 100 interviews—the sociologists Adam Reich and Peter Bearman also discovered that there were many who "do not experience working at Walmart as unjust. Many find it makes a real community. And many people find working at Walmart creative and meaningful."

Years later, I would find the same thing during my interviews with Walmart workers. "I think they're a great company," said Jack Hale, who began as a part-time hourly employee at a distribution center in Loveland, Colorado, in 1990. After holding a series of supervisory roles, he became manager of the training academy at that same site. "They have given me the opportunity to grow with the company and try different things," Hale said. Molly Lopez had a similar trajectory. She started as a cashier at a Walmart in 1989, when she was in high school, and then rose to become a $23-an-hour "people lead," overseeing training and personnel matters at a Supercenter in San Benito, Texas. "The company has been good to me," Lopez said. "The opportunity is here. It all depends on the individual if they want to do it."

But those who were down on Walmart couldn't be dismissed as outliers, either. Only about 24,000 of Walmart's worker surveys were returned out of the 43,000 the company had sent out in 2012; it is possible that many of those who didn't answer were dismayed with their jobs. And many others interviewed by Reich and Bearman complained about the dreadful pay, the paucity of hours they were given, and their supervisors' churlish behavior. I would hear these same jeremiads. It was a decidedly mixed bag.

Among the most interesting subjects in the Reich and Bearman study were those who started out satisfied and ended up sour. One of them was Nathaniel Williams, the 19-year-old hourly worker in "The Real Walmart" ad. Williams, who was from Chicago's West Side, had grown up poor. At a couple of points in his young life, his family was homeless. As soon as he was old enough to work, he went to it, but the off-the-books jobs he could find paid barely anything at all: four bucks an hour at the corner store, five at a car dealership. So when Walmart offered Williams a job at more than $8 an hour, he was so grateful to have it that he commuted two hours by bus and train to a Supercenter in the suburbs.

Williams was an exemplary employee. He eagerly took on tasks outside of his official job handling inventory in the stock room. "I had keys to the whole building," Williams said. "I moved trailers. I would train people. I would deal with customer complaints. I would do overrides. I did everything on the assistant manager's level."

When Williams appeared on TV, he thought he had a promising future at Walmart. It wasn't an act. "I am the next American success story," he said, beaming into the camera. "Working for a store where 75 percent of store management started as hourly associates—there's opportunity here! I can use Walmart's education benefits to get a degree! Maybe work in IT! Or be an engineer, helping Walmart conserve energy! When people look at me, I hope they see someone working their way up."

Within a year, Williams was out. Despite what a striver he was, he never received a promotion. Others passed him by. Williams said he never got a good answer as to why he wasn't made a manager. Maybe, he figured, "because of where I came from and my background, and because of the fact that I was so excited just to be making minimum wage, they took advantage of that." He wound up quarreling with his boss, transferring to a different store, joining OUR Walmart, and, before long, leaving the company. "It's like I've just been tossed to the curb," he said.

"If there was just a campaign...entitled 'The Real, Real Walmart,' then people would actually be able to see," Williams mused. "Like if we were to put the commercials side by side—the then and the now—there are a lot of people in this world that would be like, 'Really? So, is this what happens?' There would be a lot of people—well, there's already a lot of people protesting Walmart, but there would be a lot more."

In June 2013, the month after "The Real Walmart," debuted, Leslie Dach retired from the company. He had accomplished much during his seven years at the retailer. "He helped position them as being good—good for seniors, good for families, good for the community—and they really were perceived as bad," said Michael Robinson, executive vice president of Levick, a public relations firm in Washington.

Walmart had even softened up the White House—no small thing given what seemed to be Barack Obama's emphatic stance as a presidential candidate: "I know I won't shop there." Beyond its congruence on healthcare, the company had collaborated (or would soon collaborate) with the administration on a variety of policy priorities: hiring military veterans, fighting food insecurity, buying products made in America, combating climate change, and more. The president met with Mike Duke to talk about the national economy. And Michelle Obama, as part of her Let's Move! campaign to counter the epidemic of childhood obesity in America, ambled down the aisles of a Walmart in Missouri and gave the company kudos for its commitment to selling healthier foods.

As with many, if not most, of the programs that Dach had nurtured, there was something bona fide behind it: Walmart had used its clout in the marketplace to make fresh fruits and vegetables, as well as processed foods with less sugar and salt, more available to more people. "I hold them up as a model for taking advantage of the position that they uniquely have because of their size and because of their distribution, coupled with a willingness to do the right thing," said Jim Gavin, who served as chairman of the Partnership for a Healthier America, a nonprofit formed in conjunction with Let's Move!

Later, the president himself would head to a Walmart in Mountain View, California, using the store—with its LED lighting, green "secondary loop" refrigeration system, solar panels on the roof, and charging stations for electric vehicles in the parking lot—as a backdrop to announce new energy efficiency standards by his administration. "While we know the shift to clean energy won't happen overnight...we know that if we do, it's going to save us ultimately money and create jobs over the long term," Obama said. "That's what Walmart understands, and Walmart is pretty good at counting its pennies."

Union supporters looked upon the visit as treasonous. Robert Reich, who'd been labor secretary during the Clinton administration, said the president's appearance at Walmart came straight out of the "department of ill-advised photo opportunities." "What numbskull in the White House arranged this?" he asked. The UFCW's Joe Hansen said Obama was sending "a terrible message to workers across America."

As Dach exited the company, he expressed feeling good, having fulfilled most of his objectives. "When things are going really well, that's the right time" to step aside, he said. Mike Duke credited him with having been pivotal "in helping us understand the broader role Walmart can play in meeting the major challenges facing society today." But years later, while deconstructing his contributions to the company, Dach conceded that he had not been able to get Walmart to move in at least one area: paying its frontline workers better. "One of my frustrations was not being more successful on the wage side," Dach said. "I don't have an excuse for it. This was not one I could budge forward. I was trying. Could I have tried personally harder? Do I wish I had done it? Yeah."

While Dach packed up his office in Bentonville, OUR Walmart caravanned into town, just in time for the company's annual shareholders meeting. The organization called this latest protest the Ride for Respect, evoking the Freedom Rides of the Civil Rights Movement. Buses had left from seven different parts of the country—Washington, DC, Miami, Chicago, Dallas, Northern California, Southern California, and Seattle—picking up striking Walmart workers en route to Arkansas.

As with the prior year's Black Friday walkouts, the number of those on strike was minuscule—about 100 in all—especially when compared with the 14,000 employees that Walmart was bringing in to take part in company-sponsored celebrations, including concerts by Elton John and Luke Bryan. Still, the mustering of OUR Walmart members in Bentonville was enough to rattle executives. They requested and won from a County Circuit Court judge a temporary restraining order prohibiting OUR Walmart organizers from entering company property for "picketing, patrolling, parading, demonstrations, 'flash mobs,' handbilling, solicitation, and manager confrontations." (In the years to come, Walmart would win permanent injunctions against OUR Walmart in Arkansas, Florida, Texas, Colorado, Ohio, Maryland, and California—a rebuke of the group's unabashedly intrusive tactics.)

The order did little to slow down the protestors. For a week they took to the streets, marching and chanting. While company-approved workers amassed for a pep rally outside the Home Office, OUR Walmart members stood 50 feet away, singing, "Which side are you on Walmart.... Are you on the side of safety or on the side of murder?"—an allusion to the more than 1,200 Bangladeshi garment workers killed in a fire and building collapse at factories that had produced apparel for Walmart. Near the home of billionaire Jim Walton, Sam's youngest son, a striking worker hoisted an enlarged check for $8.81—the estimate from research firm IBISWorld of the average hourly wage the company paid. (Walmart disputed the figure.) "We are associates," Cindy Murray said. "It means equal partners. Do any of you feel equal today?"

On June 7, at the annual meeting, OUR Walmart member Janet Sparks—who had worked for the company at a store in Baker, Louisiana, for eight years and was also a shareholder—rose to speak. "Sam Walton said the goal of this company was to have customer service that was not just the best, but was legendary," she told the packed auditorium. "As a customer service manager, I try to make that goal a reality every day. We all know that times are tough for many of our customers, but I want you to know that times are tough for many Walmart associates too." Applause rippled through the audience.

"We are stretching our paychecks to pay our bills and support our families," Sparks said. "Many of us are not getting as many hours as we used to, and that makes it even harder. It also makes it hard to provide the kind of customer service that Mr. Sam expected. Now, the new associates in my store aren't even hired as permanent employees. They are hired as temps with no benefits, not even the discount card. So, when I think about the fact that our CEO, Mike Duke, made over $20 million last year, more than 1,000 times the average Walmart associate—with all due respect, I have to say, I don't think that's right."

The applause grew louder. Some cheered—a stunning outburst at a corporate pageant that Walmart normally scripted very tightly.

Sparks went on: "That $20 million you received, Mr. Duke, most of it came from bonuses. But at the store where I work, associates have only received two quarterly bonuses in the past five years. And the last one was just $26.17. As hard as we work, I think we deserve better. So do our customers. And so do our shareholders. The bonuses you and I get are supposed to be tied to the performance of our stores and our company, but we all see the understaffing of our stores, the long checkout lines, and the out-of-stocks that result. So, I want to know if you can honestly say our company is doing the best we can for customers and associates."

It was a question that many, and not just the rabble-rousers from OUR Walmart, were now asking.

About a month after Janet Sparks addressed the annual meeting, a man named Walter Loeb walked into a Walmart in Pittsfield, Massachusetts. In his late 80s, white-haired, and bespectacled, Loeb wouldn't have attracted any special notice. But what he saw sure grabbed him. "It was disturbing," he said.

If you were Walmart, Loeb was not somebody you wanted to let down. One of the industry's most esteemed advisers and observers, he'd been writing about retail for more than two decades, following 16 years as a senior analyst at Morgan Stanley and, before that, 20 years as an executive at Macy's and other chains. He knew the business inside and out, and his latest column for *Forbes* was as unforgiving as when theater critic Ben Brantley panned a Broadway show in the *Times*. Walmart was a flop.

"Everywhere I looked," Loeb wrote, "whether it was the men's, women's or juniors departments, merchandise was not well assorted by style, size, or color. There was no fashion message; and the presentation was poor—goods hung loose on separate racks in a most unattractive way. In the women's intimate apparel department there were many bras on the floor—certainly unappealing, not to mention an unsanitary condition.

"It wasn't just apparel that was in disarray," he said. "The rest of the store was also disorganized and out of stock; for example, the pharmacy area had many empty spaces on the vitamin shelves as well as in other categories. In the vacuum cleaner department, there were some machines on display—but no back-up stock to purchase; some styles were in boxes but not on display. There were many other departments in similar conditions. No surprise in such a poorly kept store, the bathrooms were both filthy and in serious need of management's attention—to me this shows the disregard management has for customers and employees—not a good message."

Then Loeb delivered a real gut punch: "What happened to this standard-setting retailer?" he asked. "Walmart always prided itself on neatness, cleanliness, and full assortments of merchandise. It was Sam Walton's creed to offer his customers the best values that were available. I walked Walmart stores with Mr. Sam many times—he cared deeply about people—he knew associates' names and often recognized loyal customers. Sam has been dead over 21 years, and unfortunately as the company has grown beyond his wildest dreams, it has become a bureaucracy."

Although his words carried special weight, Loeb was not the first to make such an assessment. Reports of empty shelves and shoddy service had plagued Walmart since at least 2011. But these woes had worsened, with more and more customers unable to find what they came into the store for, leaving them exasperated and off to shop at the competition. "If it's not on the shelf, I can't buy it," said Margaret Hancock, whose local Walmart in Delaware was short of lots of items on her shopping list, including face cream, cold medicine, bandages, mouthwash, hangers, lamps, and fabrics. "You hate to see a company self-destruct, but there are other places to go."

Walmart's troubles stemmed from outside forces, as well as its own blunders. The US economy, still making its way back from the Great Recession of 2007–2009, had been sluggish for years. The unemployment rate would remain over 7 percent for most of 2013. Labor force participation was low and poverty high. Gasoline prices were surging and payroll taxes rising, hitting households right in the pocketbook. "It's a train wreck for 80 percent of the American people, and Walmart sells to that 80 percent," retail consultant Howard Davidowitz said. Dollar stores were siphoning the most budget-conscious consumers.

With sales down, Walmart rushed to lower costs, including by cutting payroll. But it had gone too far; it was now hitting bone.

For the most part, admitted Bill Simon, the company's chief of US stores, these were "self-inflicted wounds." Shelves were bare because there simply weren't enough workers to refill them. In 2007, Walmart had an average of 338 employees per store in the United States. By 2013, that number was down to 281, causing overworked employees to race around their stores to assist customers while some areas had no service at all. "They just want to pull people left and right out of their departments to other departments because they're so understaffed," said Amanda Milligan, who had worked for seven years in the photo center at a Walmart in Franklin, Ohio.

For her and others, being chronically shorthanded made having a Walmart job less and less bearable. "Make it fair for everybody, that's what I want," Milligan said. "Fair wages, fair pay, equal work—not to go over in five different departments or do four different departments, three different departments, for the price of one." Many quit. One Walmart executive told me that for some hourly sales and customer service positions, turnover was as much as 200 percent, meaning that for every employee working in such a role, two others had left during the year. By comparison, the average churn in retail was about 75 percent.

The person most responsible for remedying all of this, along with Mike Duke, was Bill Simon. He had joined Walmart in 2006 from Brinker International, where he had led the growth of its restaurant chains, including Chili's. Before that, Simon had worked as an executive at a handful of big consumer companies, including Diageo, Cadbury Schweppes, PepsiCo, and RJR Nabisco.

With the Great Recession about to strangle the economy, he couldn't have come to Walmart at a rougher time. Simon, who liked to chug Monster energy drinks, pressed hard for growth. As head of US operations, he invested heavily in Walmart's e-commerce business and greatly expanded the number of smaller-format Neighborhood Markets, giving the retailer a larger presence in urban areas that couldn't accommodate a Supercenter. Still, Walmart's US sales continued to lag, and its weaknesses became more glaring—especially on the labor front.

Inside the company, many swore that Simon was sensitive to the needs of frontline employees. "He was very involved in trying to figure out what we could do to try to make things better for workers," said Kristin Oliver, who ran Walmart's HR department in the United States. "I saw him as an advocate and a champion." Simon was passionate, in particular, about painting Walmart as a place always ready to give people in need an entry-level job—a chance to get their foot on the first rung of a career ladder. It was in this spirit that Simon, who had served for 25 years in the US Navy and Navy Reserve, retiring as a lieutenant commander, established Walmart's job guarantee for military veterans. "Not every returning veteran wants to work in retail," he said. "But every veteran who does will have a place to go."

And yet Simon's portrayal of the opportunities Walmart provided once you started working there was not always consistent. At a 2013 retailing conference, he played up the statistic that the company promoted 160,000 people each year. Later, though, he seemed discouraged that so few could count on their first Walmart job being a launchpad within the company. "Some people took those jobs because they were the only ones available and haven't been able to figure out how to move out of that," Simon said. If Walmart employees "can go to another company and another job and make more money and develop, they'll be better. It'll be better for the economy. It'll be better for us as a business, to be quite honest, because they'll continue to advance in their economic life."

At the retail conference, Simon told the attendees that another indication of the "great job opportunities" at Walmart was that more than 475,000 of its workers earned more than $25,000 a year. But that just left the press and members of Congress to infer that the company's 525,000 other frontline employees made less than that. "There are only two places that workers get their income—they either get it from their employer or they get it from the taxpayer in the form of public assistance," said George Miller, the ranking member of the House Committee on Education and the Workforce. "That's basic economics." Speaking at a news conference on Capitol Hill that was put together by OUR Walmart, the California Democrat asked the company to meet the workers' demand for "a decent wage."

"A fair wage. A livable wage," Miller said. "I think Americans understand the power of their case. They understand it when they walk into a Walmart."

What worried Simon, actually, was that fewer consumers were doing just that: walking into a Walmart. It didn't take much to connect the dots between the company's faltering store traffic in 2013 and how it compensated its workers. "Without enough employees to get the basic work of a retail operation done—and with those on site being paid a wage so low that it is difficult to expect much in the way of pride or motivation—Walmart merchandise remains stacked on pallets in the warehouse rather than making it to the floor where customers can find the products they want," wrote Rick Ungar, another *Forbes* columnist.

The company defended its pay by pointing out that it was in line with that of other chains. "Retailing is the most competitive industry out there," Mike Duke said, "and we do pay competitive wages." Yet even if Walmart wasn't ready to accept that its miserable wages were hampering the business per se, Simon feared that the constant drumbeat of negative stories about working at Walmart was hindering the company's ability to win over new customers—something it had to do if it was going to turn around its slumping sales. As Simon and other top executives "thought about expanding into different customer segments and what we could do to revitalize growth," said Oliver, the HR chief, "they did clearly feel like it was a reputational issue" that needed to be cleaned up.

In the fall of 2013, Simon reached out to an executive named Melissa Kersey to ask her, she said, to help "change our employee reputation and our employment brand." Simon "didn't really know what the outcome" of this project would be, Kersey added, but he "drew up this problem that we need to go solve."

Her starting point was to tap into a body of research on workers' wants and needs that had been underway since 2011. Gisel Ruiz, who preceded Oliver as head of HR for Walmart's US operations and would then become chief operating officer of the US business, had encouraged the inquiry. She was hoping for some clues on how to deal with the barren shelves and other screwups that were aggravating customers, all while bearing in mind that Walmart was also experiencing the effects of a persistently anemic economy. It was, Ruiz said, "really, year over year, pressure building."

She knew Walmart's pay was one thing that needed to be examined. "There were a lot of states that were increasing their minimum wage, and so we were having conversations," Ruiz said. "Do we need to proactively do something instead of being in reactive mode?

"The low wages were just a challenge," she said. "We know as a company we're never going to have the highest wages. Retail jobs are not the highest-paid jobs in the United States. But what can we do?"

As they pondered potential answers, Ruiz instructed her team to collect data that would go far beyond the company's HR pulse surveys and other routine measuring sticks. "Rather than try to pretend that we know what's important to our associates, we need to go find out what matters to them most," said Ruiz. She also wanted to see a breakdown befitting an employer the size and scope of Walmart. "Because we have such a diverse workforce," she said, "what matters to one group doesn't necessarily matter to the next group."

Sorting it out fell to Elpida Ormanidou, who had started at Walmart in 2004 analyzing membership trends for Sam's Club before later becoming an analyst for Walmart HR. Intensely curious by nature, she liked to pop into stores, not just pore over spreadsheets. "Everywhere I traveled—even for vacation—I would talk to the cashiers and the people in the stores, and I would ask questions," she said. "I would do that for our stores, and then I would do that for the competition."

After enough of these outings, she began to pick up on something. "If you'd go into a Starbucks," said Ormanidou, who in 2016 would leave Walmart to become a data scientist at the coffee chain, "for the most part, people would say, 'Oh, I love it here. They accept me. I'm happy. I love my job.' But you would go to Walmart and everybody would complain. It's the same candidates, the same people who apply to Target and Walmart and McDonald's and Starbucks. How do we end up with the people who are not happy? Why do we end up with the people that are not as satisfied?"

Ormanidou had some instincts about investments in the workforce that Walmart would need to make if it wanted to change things. But she realized that if her ideas were going to get anywhere, she'd need to ground her case in the numbers. She was pleased, therefore, when Ruiz asked her to pull in data about what workers were looking for in a job. This, Ormanidou thought, would be the first step toward lowering turnover and, ultimately, energizing Walmart's financial returns. "There can be a win-win situation," Ormanidou said, "where the business can get what it wants and the associates can get what they want."

Under her direction, focus groups were held and surveys fielded. In total, more than 100,000 frontline employees gave their input. To add further texture to the findings, Ormanidou's head of research worked as a frontline associate at about a dozen stores in the Southeast in 2012 and 2013 in a real-life version of *Undercover Boss*.

Gustavo Canton, Ormanidou's inside man, would venture into a Walmart wearing a beat-up T-shirt, jeans, and scuffed sneakers, track down a manager, and show his company badge. His patter went something like this: "Hi, my name is Gustavo. I'm here in Atlanta and, as part of my role, I'm supporting operations. I'd like to learn better how this store functions. Is there a way I can take a shift and do whatever work is needed? I just want to learn." Sometimes, those in charge of the store would probe and discover that Canton was from HR in Bentonville; he'd never lie if asked directly. Whenever this happened, just about every employee at that location suddenly seemed to know who he was, and he wouldn't stay. But when it went well, and Canton didn't have to answer too many questions, he'd roll up his sleeves and blend right in. "They used to go, 'Who's this Hispanic guy?'" said Canton, who grew up in Panama. "Must be a new guy."

At these stores, he'd work for about two weeks—an immersion that opened Canton's eyes to many things. "I saw the good, the bad, and the ugly," he said.

He soon appreciated, as he never had before, that Walmart could be a safe haven for those whose lives were roiled by conflict or violence. "The store was the one place they were happy to come because of what might be happening in their neighborhood or their household," Canton said. "They felt at peace in the store." He witnessed employees who were big-hearted and kind. "I saw stores where the manager treated people like they were family," Canton said. "If anybody needed anything, they would do amazing things."

Yet it was also painfully evident that the need for so much generosity—managers buying their employees' groceries or covering their rent, workers splitting their sandwich with a friend who couldn't afford a meal—was a byproduct of just how hard-up many of those at Walmart were. "I saw stores where some of my fellow associates were actually stealing food," Canton said. At a Walmart in Georgia, he found out that a co-worker was sleeping in his car. Canton referred him to an employee assistance program. "I was heartbroken," he said.

After his tour, Canton wanted more than ever to help re-imagine Walmart's wage structure and scheduling. But, like Ormanidou, he understood that there was a process to follow. Arguing solely on moral grounds wouldn't get you very far. "You can either criticize the company or you can say, 'We have the belief that we can do better for our workforce, and there is a case—financial and human—that makes sense for us to move forward,'" Canton told me.

"I mean, personally speaking, I believe people should have a livable wage," he said. "I wanted this to happen tomorrow. But things don't happen that way. Sometimes, they take time. How do you justify for the business to invest? How do you justify for the business to make changes?"

In April 2013, with loads of quantitative and qualitative information having been parsed, HR completed a "segmentation study," which separated Walmart's workforce into five archetypes: newcomers to the company, whose employee "behaviors" were still taking shape; "experiential" workers, who were "influenced by how we continue to engage them," whether it was through training or mentoring; "transactional" employees, who "illustrate preference for…immediate rewards"; "legacy" associates, who "have reached a level of comfort in role and status"; and a "talent pipeline" made up of employees bound for promotion.

They desired different things. For example, those in the "legacy" and "experiential" buckets tended to want fixed schedules, while those who were new to the company or in the "transactional" category were more partial to flexible schedules. This distinction proved critical. From it, Walmart gleaned that if it wanted to meet its workers' varied needs, it had to offer both scheduling options: fixed and flexible. The study also showed that those in the "talent pipeline"—dynamos that no business wants to lose—were quitting at the second-highest rate, behind only those new to the company. A big reason for that was an absence of "development opportunities." Said Oliver: "For me, the big aha was that it's not good for either the worker or the company for people to come into entry-level jobs and stay there."

There were also common concerns. One thing that most everyone seemed to want, no matter which segment they were part of, was "competitive pay." In fact, the study found, the number one reason that people would leave Walmart was to earn more money. For many of those who decided to stay with the company, "the only thing that was keeping them there was the lack of finding something better elsewhere," said Andy Gottman, who joined the US human resources team in late 2013.

It is tempting, of course, to wonder why Walmart needed months of research to suss out that its workers wanted higher wages and schedules that fit their lives. OUR Walmart, for one, was already telling everybody that.

Yet as obvious as it may have been to OUR Walmart and the media that many of the company's workers were desperate for these things, "I don't know that anyone in leadership knew with certainty that that was the case," Gottman said. As at many large companies, the Kool-Aid that gets passed around in Bentonville can be very strong, even intoxicating. The "preexisting belief," according to Gottman, was that "we care about our associates"—no matter what some outsiders were saying. "With a million and a half people," he added, "sometimes it's hard to figure out what is real associate sentiment and what is the noise of people who may or may not have the company's best interests in mind."

But now, given the rigor that Ormanidou and her number-crunchers brought to the discussion, it was unquestionable: there was "some truth to what critics have been saying," as Gottman put it. Maybe even more than some. In any case, "we didn't spend a lot of time reflecting on who was right or who was wrong," Gottman said. "It was, 'Here's the problem laid out in front of us. Now let's go solve it.'"

In the months to come, Walmart would pilot a new scheduling system at stores around Wichita, Kansas, and a new employee development program called Pathways in Joplin, Missouri. Everything was finally coming together to make progress in the area that had eluded Leslie Dach. At last, it seemed there were brighter days ahead for Walmart's frontline workers.

Still, it would take a new face in the CEO's office to package it up and add what was arguably the most essential element of all—one that the company, going back to Sam Walton's time, had always been loath to adopt: higher wages.

CHAPTER 5

Cash

THREE DAYS BEFORE Thanksgiving 2013—or, of more consequence on the Walmart calendar, four days before Black Friday—the company announced that Mike Duke was stepping down as CEO. He would be replaced the following February by Doug McMillon.

During his five years at the helm, Duke had given Walmart "a much larger international footprint" and "a toehold in e-commerce," the *Wall Street Journal* said, leading to $65 billion in additional annual revenue. But "weakness at home," the paper concluded, had caused Walmart's stock to underperform. While the retailer's shares were up about 70 percent since Duke became CEO, the S&P 500 index had more than doubled during that same period.

Duke, who was 63, had approached Walmart's board of directors earlier in the year, saying that he was ready to retire. Many gathered that it was a two-horse race to succeed him, a choice between Bill Simon and McMillon, who was running Walmart's overseas operation and, prior to that, had spent most of his 22-year career with the company in merchandising in the United States. He'd also been president of Sam's Club from 2005 to 2009.

That the person who won out was McMillon, a Walmart lifer, rather than Simon, who had joined the company from elsewhere, was taken by many as a sign that the board was looking to stick with the same strategy (even while management corrected all the operational snafus in the stores). "I would bet that very little would be different," said Joe Feldman, a senior retail analyst at Telsey Advisory Group. Faye Landes, an analyst at Cowen & Co., predicted, "He's a Walmart guy from Arkansas, so I would be shocked to see dramatic changes in how the company is run."

In fact, McMillon would bring a strong sense of continuity to the CEO job. Although he was just 47 years old, he was as much a creature of Walmart's customs and conventions as anyone who had ever occupied Sam Walton's old office—in many respects, even more so.

For most of his young life, McMillon was raised in Jonesboro, Arkansas. His father was a dentist, and his mother helped run the practice. The family lived comfortably, but modestly. "Dad would chuckle and say, 'I never charged enough for my services,'" McMillon told me. "We probably were middle-class, but we might've lived one click below that because of his mentality related to savings. My dad and my mom, neither one of them grew up with any money. They were very conservative and focused on savings. So we certainly didn't live like we were wealthy, but I didn't want for anything, either."

When McMillon was a toddler, his mom would shop at Gibson's Discount Center. Then in 1971, when he was five, a Walmart came to town. "It changed how we shopped, and I think changed how a bunch of people shopped," he said. "One of my memories is of my mom going out on Saturday. And as she was leaving, she would say, 'I'm going to Walmart. What do you need?' Later on, it sunk in with me that she didn't say, 'I'm going shopping' or 'I'm going to the grocery store.' She would say, 'I'm making a Walmart run' or 'I'm going to Walmart.' And to me, that...just brought to life what Sam originally intended as he was working on the discount store model. You just stop thinking about where you're going to shop because Walmart had the assortment and quality at low prices. It became the default for shopping."

Between McMillon's sophomore and junior year of high school, his father moved his dental practice to Bentonville. Being uprooted is never easy for a teenager, but McMillon was a good basketball player, and he became the point guard for Bentonville High. That helped ease the transition.

He also worked—not that he had any choice in the matter. "My dad picked cotton to help pay his way through school and was convinced that I needed to pay my own way through school, regardless of whether he could help or not," McMillon said. "I was encouraged to save my money for college but also cover my own expenses to the extent possible." When he first got to Bentonville, he drove around in his Honda Civic, with his push mower poking out the back, and cut lawns. But he wanted something steadier. His options came down to a McDonald's, which paid $3.35 an hour, and a Walmart distribution center, which paid $6.50. (He'd also applied to a Kraft Foods factory in Bentonville but never heard back.)

In the summer of 1984, McMillon took a job unloading trucks at the Walmart warehouse. He got off to a bad start. Really bad. Not even an hour into his first day of work, McMillon's boss asked him and some others to head over to the high school gym to help set up the space for Walmart's annual shareholder meeting. On his way, McMillon switched on the portable cassette player he kept on the front seat beside him; because the Civic had no radio, he'd blast ZZ Top and Loverboy on the boom box. At a stop sign, he thought he better turn down the music and got so distracted that he rolled forward and knocked right into the rear bumper of his boss's car. Thankfully, there was no damage—except, momentarily, to McMillon's self-assurance.

"McMillon, you're not very smart, are you?" his boss said.

"Apparently not, sir," he answered.

More than 20 years later, when he had become CEO, McMillon would turn the slip-up into a leadership parable. After his boss climbed back into his car, McMillon told the 2021 graduating class of Harvard Business School, he never said another word about having been hit. "Please remember to give people grace on the small stuff," McMillon advised the graduates.

There would be other takeaways for McMillon, as well. To an outsider, these recollections could come across as pure puffery. But it was difficult, in speaking with him, not to find McMillon totally sincere; even when reciting the most saccharine story about Walmart, he exuded authenticity. "The thing that stuck with me more than anything else about that first summer," he said, "was how happy people were and how excited they were about the company. There was this one guy—I don't know his last name, but his first name was Johnny. I was unloading a truck with Johnny one day, and he had his shirt off, and we're both sweating and working hard. He was telling me how great his experience was at Walmart....He told me he had—I think I've got the number right—$200,000 in profit sharing already at that point. For him and his life, $200,000 was a lot of money. So, Johnny was like, 'This is a great place to work and we're growing. And this is awesome for me.' And so, to have somebody when the temperature is probably 100-plus be so happy, that left an impression."

McMillon worked the following summer at a Walmart returns center in the neighboring town of Rogers. As he popped open one trailer after another, he was struck by the large volume of abused items that had been shipped back—busted bikes, broken fishing rods, and smashed aquariums. Some of them were affixed with labels from Kmart or Sears; they hadn't even been purchased at Walmart in the first place. "It was like, 'Wow, our store managers are taking anything. Is that good business? Is that smart?' But you know, it was brilliant. 'Satisfaction guaranteed' was one of the reasons why people like my mom said, 'I'm going to Walmart.'"

McMillon went on to pursue his undergraduate degree at the University of Arkansas in Fayetteville, about a half-hour from Bentonville. During school, he worked at a bank owned by a Walton-controlled holding company called Arvest. One year, during the holidays, he even got to park cars at Sam and

Helen's Christmas party. (Evidently, nobody told them about his rear-ender back in high school.) The evening gave McMillon a glimpse into their thrift as much as their wealth. As it got dark, Helen asked McMillon to come inside the house so that she could grab a flashlight for him and the other parking attendants. When she opened the cabinet, it was stuffed with boxes of Kleenex.

"Ms. Walton, you sure do have a lot of Kleenex," McMillon said.

"They had a deal down at Sam's Club," she replied. "I bought the whole pallet."

The main thing McMillon learned from his time at the bank was that he didn't like banking. As he neared graduation, he had a chance to be put on a management track at Arvest. He turned it down. "I think I need something a little faster," McMillon told Burt Stacy, the president. As an immediate next step, McMillon added, he planned to get his MBA at the University of Tulsa. Stacy then did McMillon one of the biggest favors of his life.

"Well, before you leave town," Stacy said, "I think it'd be smart for you to go meet somebody at Walmart. If you're not going to work for Arvest, I can arrange an interview for you so that somebody at Walmart really knows who you are before you go off to school."

McMillon was jazzed. He had enjoyed his summer jobs at Walmart while in high school. Moreover, in college he had started dating the woman who would become his wife, and she was a teacher in Bentonville. His parents still lived there too. As McMillon told Bill Fields, the company's chief merchant with whom Stacy had set up the meeting, Walmart seemed like it would be the ideal place for him when he finished his MBA. Fields agreed that he'd be well-suited for the company's buyer-training program.

Before his second year, McMillon called Fields to let him know that he was still interested in a job at Walmart—as soon as his diploma was in hand. But Fields had a different timetable in mind. He told McMillon that he could get started right away at Walmart No. 894 in Tulsa.

"Bill, I can't do that," McMillon said. "I'm taking a lot of hours here. My MBA is a full-time deal. I'm a graduate assistant. I'm working for the University of Tulsa to help pay my way through school."

"No," Fields said, "you can do it. I'll tell them you'll be there at seven o'clock."

McMillon didn't disappoint. He became an assistant manager, juggling 50-plus hours a week at the store plus his MBA. Walmart was, in many ways, his actual education. "I figured out pretty quickly that the people who really ran that store were the department managers," McMillon said. "They looked at you like, 'Are you going to be some college kid who walks in here the first day, trying to tell me what to do? Or are you going to be smart about this and let me teach you something?' Cashiers turned over. But the people on the sales floor, they were tenured, and they could teach you something about how to sell merchandise, how to serve customers."

McMillon relished the work, and after completing school in 1991 he returned to Bentonville to become a merchant in the Home Office, picking which products Walmart would stock. He started in sporting goods. On McMillon's first day, he found a note on his desk pointing out that Kmart was selling a type of fishing line for less than Walmart was. McMillon wasn't sure who had written it, so he showed it to his boss, who in an instant recognized that the red flag had come from Sam Walton himself. McMillon lowered the price and took in a valuable lesson: to survive in retail, you must stay on top of the nitty-gritty and act swiftly and decisively.

Soon, McMillon would appreciate not only Mr. Sam's sharp eye but also his quick wit. At Walmart's weekly Saturday morning meeting at the Home Office—once described by *Fortune* as "equal parts talk show, financial update, encounter group, merchandising workshop, town-hall forum, talent revue, gripe session, and, of course, pep rally"—McMillon stood at the end of the line, about to make his maiden presentation. He had just scored a coup by coaxing the maker of a fishing product called Baitmate to roll back its price while allowing Walmart to maintain its margin. McMillon summarized the art of the deal: "They'd taught me to say, 'I'm a new buyer, and I could be here a long time. So, would you mind giving me a lower price and get me started on the right foot? I won't forget it.'" The Baitmate salesman bit.

As he got ready to go to bat for the "fish attractant"—it uses natural oils to give off an odor that, when sprayed on a lure, is a magnet for different freshwater and saltwater species—McMillon went through the fine points one more time in his head: the price, the number of units sold, all the scents that the product came in. As Mr. Sam held a microphone in front of McMillon's face, the fledgling merchant displayed a bottle of Baitmate to the room. McMillon was so nervous, his hand shook. His voice quavered. Then, as he finished, Walton weighed in, deadpan.

"That's all well and good, son," Mr. Sam said, "but what makes you think fish can smell?"

Laughter filled the auditorium, and McMillon slunk to his seat. He'd have a few more interactions with Walton before the icon passed away the next year, but it wasn't like the two were close. Back then, said McMillon, "I was just a young buyer in the organization and probably not worth knowing."

His status rose rapidly. McMillon was adept at sorting out merchandising areas that were bogged down with too much inventory or were having other hiccups, and so he was sent from one to another—food, women's wear, crafts and fabrics, furniture, infants and toddlers—as a kind of Mr. Fix-It.

"The whole challenge of being a merchant was so fun," McMillon said. "You never stop learning. It's moving all the time in big and small ways. There's a risk associated with buying a new item. But if you don't buy a new item, you're boring and you won't have any sales growth. So the idea of working with a supplier community and figuring out how to take everything they're trying to sell you and put it into the space that you're given in the store to optimize sales and profit is a huge business challenge. And you get involved in supply chain and marketing and store operations. You have to know what a store associate's job is like because you need them. You're right in the middle of it all."

In short, becoming a merchant made McMillon feel that he was doing something important—that he had taken on responsibility for what made Walmart Walmart. "We call them buyers, but if it doesn't sell, you don't get to be a buyer very long," he said. "So really, you're a seller. That's what it comes down to. Can you grow sales?"

At department meetings, buyers armed with calculators and yellow legal pads would tangle over who deserved more promotional dollars and, by extension, who among the others around the table deserved fewer. "Doug was in the fray," said Don Harris, one of McMillon's first supervisors and his biggest influence in his early years at the company. "He embraced it. You saw the gleam when he started." (Harris had the perfect pedigree to help groom McMillon; his father, Claude, had been a partner of Sam Walton's and became Walmart's first buyer in 1968.)

Thirty years later, as CEO, McMillon's official corporate bio would still include the line: "He remains a merchant at heart." I could see it myself as the two of us traversed a Supercenter in Lake Elsinore, California, in the spring of 2021—part of a series of usually unannounced, weekly check-ins that McMillon makes at US stores and in other markets when he's traveling internationally.

Near the entrance, boxes of coconut water—everyday low price: 98 cents—lined the wall. A two-liter bottle of Sam's Cola fetched 74 cents. "We want you to immediately see the value," McMillon said. Ahead, a bright selection of fruits and vegetables marked a gateway to the grocery, while computers and eyeglasses and a panoply of other goods fanned out to our right. The entire flow of the store, McMillon said, had been put together to "distribute you around the building, to shop the whole box."

As we got to the coffee makers, you could see the company's strategy at play: there was a Mainstays brand for $9.88—just right for someone on a small budget—and a Ninja espresso machine for $129. "We've had to work hard to not lose the traditional customer," McMillon said, while also appealing to consumers who might have more disposable income.

He was exhilarated by the puzzle of it all. "I love this thing!" McMillon said as we inspected the back room, stacked with wares waiting to be taken to the sales floor. "It's so cool—this whole business."

McMillon's prowess as a merchant catapulted him into Walmart's executive ranks. As a senior vice president, he led the charge into electronics. "Flat-screen TVs were just hitting," said Don Harris, who had become head of general merchandise for the company's US stores. "Doug pushed his electronics division to just—bam!—let's take the whole back wall of the store, and let's make it happen. And let's see if we can figure out a way to do business with Apple.

"It's this notion of pushing forward, saying, 'What's next? What's new? What's trending? What can we do? What can we take advantage of? What kind of resources do we need?' Doug always had that knack."

He stood apart in other ways, as well. A. G. Lafley, the former CEO of Procter & Gamble, a key Walmart supplier, communicated frequently with executives at the retailer. Most of them "would call you when they needed something" to facilitate the business, Lafley said. "Doug was a little different. He would engage you when he was curious about something, when he wanted to learn something that he thought you might know about or had some experience with. I viewed that as a real indicator of somebody who will keep growing."

When he was only 38, McMillon became the CEO of Sam's Club—a business so large that had it been a stand-alone enterprise, it would have ranked as the 41st biggest company in America at the time (bigger than Microsoft or Lockheed, Intel, or Allstate). His appointment as head of Walmart International in 2009 gave him senior leadership experience in each of the company's business segments.

Yet even though McMillon had been made by Walmart, the Wall Street analysts who'd inferred that this personal history foreshadowed a stay-the-course sensibility were dead wrong. Sure, he would proudly preserve the corporation's heritage. But when it came to the business, he wasn't about to stand still—a characteristic that was itself Walmart born and bred. "One of the greatest strengths of Walmart's ingrained culture," Sam Walton had postulated, "is its ability to drop everything and turn on a dime." Mr. Sam went on to say that "you can't just keep doing what works . . . because everything around you is always changing. To succeed, you have to stay out in front of that change." The analysts had overlooked how hard-wired that attitude would be in someone like Doug McMillon.

When McMillon became CEO, one of the first things he did was give every member of his executive team a copy of Brad Stone's 2013 book about Amazon, *The Everything Store*. It wasn't optional reading. "I felt that our leadership wasn't as focused on our biggest competitive threat as they should have been," McMillon told me. "It's so easy at Walmart to get focused on a long list of retail competitors. I was trying to cut through that noise a bit and say, 'If there's one competitor that we should be learning from right now, because of how customers are responding to them, it's this one. And this one is different. Amazon is not Aldi. Amazon is not Kroger. Amazon is not Costco. It's something different. And I want to get your focus on that.'"

The Everything Store details Amazon's rise from a simple bookseller, when its site went live to the buying public in 1995, to an online giant whose sales would increase from less than $10 billion to more than $100 billion in only a decade. Not surprisingly, Walmart appears throughout. In late 2000, the companies even flirted, according to Stone. Amazon founder Jeff Bezos and a couple of his executives flew to Bentonville to explore whether Amazon might handle Walmart's e-commerce business, while Lee Scott gently floated the idea of Walmart acquiring Amazon. "The conversation between the two retailers remained a quirk of history," Stone writes, "a tantalizing suggestion of what might have been. The two companies would continue on separate paths, which, years later, would converge to produce a fierce rivalry."

Indeed, by 2010, fierce was an understatement. Stone pieces together how that year, Amazon outmaneuvered Walmart to buy Quidsi, the parent company of Diapers.com. As the two companies issued bids and counterbids, Amazon let it be known that if it lost out to Walmart, it would "drive diaper prices to zero" at its own online marketplace, potentially wiping out any competition. "The Quidsi board convened to discuss the Amazon proposal and the possibility of letting it expire and then resuming negotiations with Walmart," Stone writes. "But by then, Bezos's Khrushchev-like willingness to take the e-commerce equivalent of the thermonuclear option in the diaper price war made Quidsi worried that it would be exposed and vulnerable if something went wrong during the consummation of a shotgun marriage to Walmart. So the Quidsi executives stuck with Amazon, largely out of fear."

I asked McMillon what the most essential insight was that he and the other Walmart executives got out of *The Everything Store*. "You learn something about mindset," he said. "I think one of the words from the book that people focused on was 'relentless.'"

For all the attention that Amazon warranted, McMillon was careful. He didn't want his team to "get over-infatuated" with any individual rival and develop tunnel-vision. "Amazon's done an incredible job," he said, "but H-E-B is really good at fresh food. And Publix is doing a great job in Florida, and Wegmans does a better job in fresh food in the Northeast than we do. Costco is an amazing retailer. And so, the philosophy that Walmart has—and I've been taught from the beginning—is study the best of the best on everything and apply what you should apply for your business. We cannot become another company and shouldn't try. We should be a better Walmart. But we can take great ideas. And no doubt, Amazon has generated a lot of demand from customers and done a lot of great things, and we can learn from those."

McMillon has a way of connecting with people—whether it's a fellow CEO or an employee on the front lines. He is gracious and personable. He's a very good listener. His emotional intelligence is extremely high. But it would be a mistake to think, because of these traits, that he lacks a killer instinct. In truth, said the *Financial Times*, he is "a soft-spoken Southern charmer—but one with a hard edge."

Don Harris had seen it flare before. Once, when he and McMillon had a little free time during a toy-buying trip to Hong Kong, they played pickup basketball with some locals at an outdoor court. The two Americans guarded each other. It was a friendly, slow-paced game—until about halfway in. "I started getting up in his grill on defense a little bit, trying to get a chest on him," Harris said. "And he flipped the switch." In a scene reminiscent of the way that Sam Walton used to play tennis, McMillon dominated from that moment on, destroying Harris and taking down the other team. "He is mild-mannered," Harris said, "but he's got a competitive gene."

Within a year of his being in the top job, the notion that McMillon was content to be a status-quo CEO had vanished. *Fortune* now declared him "the man who's reinventing Walmart." Under his direction, the company would, in time, winnow its foreign presence; buy the e-commerce site Jet.com for more than $3 billion—and then shut it down; otherwise rev up its online business by introducing new services and expanding its stable of third-party sellers; unveil a subscription program, akin to Amazon Prime, called Walmart+; build local fulfillment centers—compact warehouses powered by robotics and artificial intelligence—right in its stores; dive into digital advertising; cultivate customers on TikTok, the viral video app; venture into the metaverse and the worlds of cryptocurrency and nonfungible tokens; deliver products by drone and driverless truck; put groceries right into people's fridges while they weren't home; open health clinics and offer medical insurance; launch a financial technology startup; buy the menswear company Bonobos; buy and sell the women's apparel company ModCloth; beef up its fashion brands by hiring a creative director, Brandon Maxwell, who, as *Vogue* observed, was in a coterie of designers who typically took on engagements in Paris or Milan, not Bentonville; and much, much more. "I can't remember a time when there was so much exciting change happening inside our company," McMillon would come to say.

Yet before any of this could occur, the CEO knew he had to tackle first things first: assuaging the discontent of his frontline employees.

Still Broke

In July 2014, Walmart said that Bill Simon was leaving the company. The new head of US operations would be Greg Foran, who'd led the retailer's business in China for the previous two years.

Some had expected Simon to depart; once Doug McMillon was named CEO, they presumed, it was only a matter of time before the runner-up would move along. McMillon, in a statement, commended Simon for "his passion for our mission, dedication to our associates and our customers, and innovative thinking," which had resulted in Walmart's $4 prescription program, smaller-format stores, and the blending of digital and physical retailing. Others were less kind, citing five straight quarters—soon to be six—of declining sales at Walmart's US stores. "Leaders that don't deliver over time should be replaced, and Simon has not delivered," George Bradt wrote in *Forbes*. Walter Loeb's assessment of Simon's exit began this way: "It is about time."

Foran had gotten his start in retail in the 1970s, packing supermarket shelves in his native New Zealand. He came to Walmart in 2011 after being passed over as CEO of Woolworths in Australia. Because he'd never worked in the United States, some were unsettled that Walmart would now put him in charge of its flagship division. "Foran," *Chain Store Age* said, "represents a real wild card." But McMillon had watched Foran in China and knew that he intuitively grasped how to get Walmart's low-cost, low-price flywheel spinning. "Greatest retailer on the planet," McMillon would say of him.

By late 2014, as Foran and his new team began to travel to stores throughout the US, they discovered that things were in far worse shape than they had imagined. Even while sales were slipping, profits had held up for the most part, masking the seriousness of Walmart's infirmities. "Profit can hide many sins," Foran said. "Each rock I turned over indicated that our business was past its prime."

At many locations, unsold merchandise had piled up so much, "you couldn't actually get into the back room," said Judith McKenna, who had become Foran's chief operating officer. "There was so much inventory in there that you had one door you could go in and out of, but you couldn't get all the way through to come out" the door on the other side. Some stores started cramming items into trailers outside the store until they, too, became so jam-packed that they were mostly inaccessible.

There was no single cause of the chaos. Some of it was due to the best managers being pulled out of Supercenters and into new Neighborhood Markets. "You had this talent drain," McKenna said. There was also the underinvestment in labor, which had left stores with too few frontline workers. Even now, managers complained that they weren't being permitted to add more staffing to complete basic tasks. One analyst report said that if Walmart's payroll had kept up with its growth in square footage, as it should have, the company would have 1.5 million US workers—200,000 more than it did then. Those who were on the job, meanwhile, were hamstrung by an overly complex system for getting products where they needed to go. "Our process to put something on the shelf was seven steps," said Darren Carithers, who worked with Foran and McKenna as vice president of central operations. You practically "had to be an engineer to get it right."

Compounding the situation was a profusion of promos meant to resuscitate the US business. Having Wednesday or Sunday specials—a tactic common to other retailers—ran counter to Walmart's credo of providing "everyday low prices" across the board. Under EDLP, as it's known, Walmart strives to build trust with its customers because they know they will always get the best available prices for a full basket of goods and won't come back the next day or the next week only to find that they missed a markdown. What's more, operational and cost efficiencies throughout the supply chain and in the store can be achieved because there aren't spikes in demand for certain products for limited amounts of time.

Yet under Simon, specially advertised items were being consigned on a weekly basis to the stores. The problem was that whatever didn't sell wound up in the back room—and a lot didn't sell. After a while, store managers were "operating on their instincts," McKenna said. "It was almost like survival." With stock literally lost inside the store, they began to manually bypass the normal ordering system for merchandise in the hope, McKenna said, that "I can get my hands on it because I'll know where it is." However, many of these items didn't sell, either. They'd be returned to the back room, as well, adding to the mountain of clutter. "It created a doom loop," Carithers said.

As they made the rounds, Foran and McKenna also saw how much employees' long-festering concerns about low pay and erratic hours were exacerbating Walmart's troubles. Coupled with the stress brought on by the logjam of inventory, work for many had become insufferable. "I went into a store in North Carolina, and their turnover was 400 percent," McKenna said. "I can remember talking to the store manager, and I was like,

'Your entire team turns over four times a year. How do you run the store?' He's like, 'I just do my best.'"

Sometimes, little things said a lot. When McKenna stepped into a store in New Mexico, she found herself staring at the floor.

"When did we start using brown tiles?" she asked Carithers.

"That's dirt," he said, "not floor tile."

As she continued to tour stores, McKenna realized this level of apathy wasn't an aberration. "Everywhere," she said, "the associates were just like, 'Nobody cares.'"

As Foran and McKenna got their arms around the worrisome condition of Walmart's US stores, the group that had investigated workers' priorities under Bill Simon was testing solutions—though they ran into some pushback. Andy Gottman, who was trying to refine Walmart's scheduling system, was confronted by store operators who were "skeptical about how much these changes would actually impact turnover." The general feeling, he said, was that "we already treat our people well, and so these changes will only hurt us; it won't help them." Added Gustavo Canton, who'd returned from his undercover expedition with all of those heart-rending stories of frontline workers unable to buy food or pay rent: "Even within my team, there was resistance to support some of these changes. Some of my PhDs are looking at it from a financial standpoint....'Look at all this microeconomic data. Look at the market. Here's competition. How do we know this is going to truly be effective and bring additional value to the company?'"

Despite the doubters, the scheduling and training pilots were now well underway. And new research was being conducted into what it would take to improve frontline retail jobs not only at Walmart but across the industry.

The executive who thought the most about how to integrate what the company was trying to do with the needs of the wider world was Kathleen McLaughlin, who carried two titles: president of the Walmart Foundation and chief sustainability officer for the company. She had assumed these posts in October 2013, a few months before McMillon became CEO, after a 23-year career at McKinsey & Company, the consulting firm.

The outgoing foundation president, Sylvia Mathews Burwell, an old college friend of McLaughlin's who was leaving Walmart to become secretary of Health and Human Services for President Obama, had urged her to take the job. Initially, McLaughlin was doubtful that Walmart was right for her. At McKinsey, she had advised many of its retail competitors, and so she was a little jaundiced about the company. "I didn't think that highly of them," she said. Her conception of how Walmart treated its hourly workers—an area that she cared about, in particular—was "not too good."

Nonetheless, she decided to check it out—"When else will I ever go to Bentonville?" she wondered—and, to her surprise, she was impressed with most everything she heard. She met with Mike Duke and Dan Bartlett, a former counselor to President George W. Bush who'd replaced Leslie Dach, and was elated by their plans to more closely mesh the work of the foundation with the company's core business strategy. At McKinsey, she'd led projects in both the corporate and social sectors; the prospect of straddling them at Walmart was thrilling. She met with Bill Simon and was heartened when he talked about trying to make things better for Walmart's frontline workers. Flying back from Bentonville to Toronto, where she lived, McLaughlin jotted down in her notebook all of the areas she would have a major hand in: "opportunity, sustainability, community, business, philanthropy." She was smitten.

When she got to the company, McLaughlin wasted no time in trying to help the leadership team turn things around, starting with the employees. "The morale was low, and they knew it," she said. "It was very poignant. I remember Bill saying, 'Look. I have to think that if someone is working for us full time, they're giving us the better part of their life. We have to do more for them.'" She also believed, based on studies she had done at McKinsey, that higher wages could raise worker productivity and, over the long run, more than pay for themselves. But with sales in the doldrums, she understood why there was some hesitancy to increase compensation. "What do you do?" she asked. "Do you take a leap and do it anyway, knowing you're going to get hammered because you don't have the sales? What comes first? The chicken or the egg? They were really struggling with that."

As the months went by, McLaughlin's staff concentrated on what training should look like, steered by the view that as workers gained new competencies—especially those that would help them prepare for a more digitized, automated workplace of the future—they'd merit additional pay. "We were thinking about how training converts to a higher wage," said Julie Gehrki, then a senior director at the foundation. There was a "real belief that we needed to tie skill and wage."

But as they elicited the advice of labor market experts and worker advocates—asking for their input in much the same way that Walmart had sought out top-notch environmentalists—some openly told them that their orientation was off. With the company's pay so low, raising wages should be the first order of business. Gehrki, for one, got an earful from Byron Auguste, an old McKinsey colleague of McLaughlin's who was now deputy director of the National Economic Council at the White House. "They would always want to come to us with their training and the upskilling stuff," Auguste recalled. "And I'd say, look, this is good directionally, but you need to understand that until you raise your minimum wage, no one's going to hear this. People will just be very cynical about it and say, 'Well, yeah, but like pay your workers more.'"

Gayatri Agnew got the same feedback. She became a director at the foundation in the fall of 2014, keen on being a change agent across the company. Her commitment was deep-seated. Agnew had grown up in public housing in East Palo Alto, California, with her sister and mother, who was divorced. Money was so hard to come by, "it was dollar to dollar, not paycheck to paycheck," Agnew said. Then, when Agnew was 12, her mom got hired as a kindergarten teacher. "That job, which was salaried and had healthcare, changed my life," she said. "We could now buy clothes—at the Goodwill, but we could buy them." Seeing the difference that a decent job made for her family would become Agnew's lodestar. "That's why I do the work that I do," she said, "and that's what brought me to Walmart."

She almost didn't come. After high school, Agnew went to college on a scholarship. The only times she got near a Walmart, she was brandishing a protest sign. "I grew up on the West Coast," she said. "I'm a liberal. I spent a lot of time with labor organizers, and so if you were fighting against injustice, you were fighting against Walmart. It was like breathing." Upon graduation, Agnew became a special assistant to Christine Gregoire, the Democratic governor of Washington. She'd later work in higher education and at several nonprofits. Walmart was the last place she could ever see herself. "I hated everything about Walmart," Agnew said. "It didn't dawn on me that Walmart was a place where change could be made."

When the recruiter from Walmart called, Agnew ignored her. But the recruiter was dogged, and finally, after the third attempt, Agnew felt so guilty about ducking her that she got in touch. Before Agnew knew it, she was on the phone with Gehrki hearing about the considerable role the foundation had in rethinking the complexion of frontline work at Walmart. "We were just having such a great conversation, and I was feeling like such an asshole for hating this company so hard for so long," Agnew said. "Here I was having this really rich dialogue with this woman who clearly cares about the world, is a good person, wants to make a difference—and she works there."

At some point, Agnew interjected. "Hey, before we go any further with this," she said, "I feel like you need to know that I protested against your company when I was in high school and college." Gehrki was unfazed. "We need you to come help us," she told Agnew.

One of Agnew's first assignments was to talk with Maureen Conway of the Aspen Institute. Like Auguste, Conway tried to emphasize that training workers could be beneficial—for them and for the company—but it was no substitute for paying people what they needed to live on. "You have to think about economic stability and not just economic mobility," said Conway, who in April 2014 had coauthored a paper on the topic. In it, she made the case that policymakers and business executives had become so enamored with trying to move low-paid workers into good jobs—as employees attained new skills—that they weren't doing enough to bring the bad jobs up to snuff.

What was necessary, Conway wrote, was "a combination of policy and practice interventions that simultaneously build ladders to assist career development and raise the floor to make poor-quality jobs better." As for Walmart, she said, "I pushed them on this."

Others did too. Since 2006, under Lee Scott, Walmart executives had met regularly with a paid panel of external advisers on workforce matters. The current incarnation of the council included the Reverend Al Sharpton; Charles Kamasaki, a senior official at the National Council of La Raza; and Alexis Herman, who'd succeeded Robert Reich as President Clinton's labor secretary. "They were helping guide us through our choices, what would make the biggest impact, because we did come to the realization that we have a social responsibility from an employee perspective," said Melissa Kersey, then a senior vice president for human resources strategy and training. "If we have only a certain number of dollars to invest, what is the best way, not just from a reputational perspective but from a societal perspective?"

On wages, however, Walmart tended to retreat to its familiar position: *C'mon, we're not bad; we pay what most retailers pay.* Kamasaki demurred. "But you have agency here, right?" he asked. "You're the biggest retailer, right? It's not like you're a mom-and-pop. You've got some ability to move the market." Herman put things in an even bigger context. For months, President Obama had been asking Congress to raise the minimum wage from \$7.25 an hour to \$10.10. "This is a very simple issue," the president said. "Either you're in favor of raising wages for hardworking Americans, or you're not. Either you want to grow the economy from the middle out and the bottom up so that prosperity is broad-based, or you think that top-down economics is the way to go." Herman told Walmart that, as the largest employer in America, it could help swing the debate in Washington if it increased its starting wage to $10 or more. "My frame was, you could be a real leader in the national dialogue," she said. "You could help shape and move things because of who you are."

She wouldn't be the last one to make this point. Valerie Jarrett, one of President Obama's closest aides, came to Bentonville and met with McMillon at the Home Office. The two of them sat alone in the Quail Room, with photos of quarry from Mr. Sam's bird hunts hanging on the wall. "She specifically said, 'It would be great if you could get your wages up to $10 an hour,'" McMillon told me.

If anyone represented an even higher authority than did Jarrett it was the members of another organization always ready to admonish Walmart: the Interfaith Center on Corporate Responsibility. Made up of hundreds of religious institutions whose pension funds and other investment accounts held stock in some of the world's biggest corporations, ICCR had been in a running discourse with the retailer since the early 1990s on a wide variety of subjects. These included executive compensation, diversity, the environment, affordable healthcare, labor standards for suppliers, product safety, gun sales, and more. For many years, "we were the only group they were talking to," said David Schilling, a senior program director at ICCR. "We were sort of pioneers in getting issues on the agenda that they didn't want to look at."

As much as any company, Walmart was predisposed to at least listen to ICCR. Although Walmart has never explicitly claimed any religious identity, an undercurrent of devoutness has long run beneath the surface. "I can unequivocally say that Sam founded the company on the Judeo-Christian principles found in the Bible," remarked Don Soderquist, the former chief operating officer. In Walmart's early days, gospel singers would perform in stores. In the 1980s, a professor from Abilene Christian University drew on evangelical teachings to counsel Walmart employees on their personal lives. As late as 1991, at the company's annual meeting, a group of Walmart truckers belted out the song "Jesus, Hold My Hand." McMillon, while taking great care to foster an inclusive workplace, has said of his own life goals: "I would like to be known as a person of faith, faith in Jesus Christ." He has peppered speeches with "God is good."

ICCR's "Walmart caucus," as it called itself, was led by Sister Barbara Aires, a firecracker of a nun from the Sisters of Charity of Saint Elizabeth in Convent Station, New Jersey. "Sister Barbara kept us on the straight and narrow in terms of her view about what we were doing," said Kristin Oliver, the HR chief for the US. "It wasn't always easy to hear, but she helped us understand the role we played in the world."

Trying to get Walmart to bump its wages had been an aim of ICCR's since a delegation met with Lee Scott shortly before he became CEO. Sister Susan Mika of the Benedictine Sisters of Boerne, Texas, told him about interviewing Walmart workers in San Antonio who earned so little that they couldn't afford to buy school supplies for their children.

As he got up to leave, Scott walked over to the other end of the long table where Mika was sitting. He got right in her face.

"I hope you don't believe what you just said," he told her, his voice rising.

Mika was startled. "Of course I believe what I said."

Aires then swooped in. "Look, Mr. Scott," she told him. "This is a meeting to discuss things where you know we disagree with you. If you can't be civil, then get out."

The relationship got much smoother from there. Scott gave Aires his cell phone number, and the two developed a good rapport. Aires could be stern. "She's a force unto herself," said Margaret Weber, the corporate responsibility coordinator for the Basilian Fathers of Toronto. But she also liked to laugh and make others laugh. She could talk about spirituality, but also sports. She would chew out the CEO or, in a small act of grace, call just to ask how he and his family were doing. "She'll say some things that are kind of strong," said Frank Rauscher of Aquinas Associates, a consultancy to Catholic institutional investors, "but then give a loving hug at the end of the reprimand."

As the dialogue continued, those in ICCR were buoyed by Walmart's progress in any number of areas. On the environment, for instance, "they've just upped their ante," Aires said. "Every year they move to a different level to address something else." But wages were one place where the company was reluctant to do anything. "You want the best for the workers," Aires said. "I mean, that was my plea. We were worried about them. We were worried about their families. We were worried about their children, worried about the number of people who work there who are single parents."

When McMillon became CEO, the members of ICCR found him more open than Lee Scott or Mike Duke to considering whatever they broached. He "doesn't have a kneejerk defensive reaction to a lot of the things that are brought up," Schilling said. And so, during 2014, "we pushed him hard, saying, 'You know, nobody can live on the salary you're paying,'" the Reverend Seamus Finn recounted.

One of ICCR's arguments was that employers such as Walmart had driven wages so low, it was causing the whole economy to hollow out. The question became: "What are you doing with your employees to make sure that we don't lose the middle class?" said Frank Sherman, executive director of an investor coalition called Seventh Generation Interfaith, who was also part of the Walmart caucus. "We were bringing a little bit of the Henry Ford."

In 1914, Ford had famously doubled his workers' pay to $5 a day, which led to much higher productivity and lower turnover. Yet Ford's raise had wider ramifications, as well. "Prosperous workers begat a prosperous marketplace, which in turn spawned more prosperous companies and in time the result was a new, conspicuously consumer-based economy," Douglas Brinkley, the historian, has written. As the Roaring Twenties gave way to the Great Depression, some wished even more companies had followed Ford. "If profits had been distributed in wages, prosperity would have been maintained and increased," the publishing baron William Randolph Hearst said in 1930. Others were of the same mind. "Low wages...are as bad for employers as they are for employees," said Edward Filene, the department store magnate, in 1936.

As World War II raged, the economy boomed. But the same logic about consumers held. "How am I going to sell my refrigerators if we don't give 'em wages to buy with?" General Electric President Charlie Wilson asked in 1944. After the war, it was more of the same. When *Time* magazine named General Motors President Harlow Curtice its Man of the Year in 1955, it highlighted the impressive wage gains made by GM workers.

"People have got money," the head of the largest department store in Flint, Michigan, told *Time*. "They feel safe." GE exalted the era as one of "people's capitalism," with hallmarks that included "high wages, high productivity, high purchasing power."

But that was then. Now, the US economy was trapped in "a vicious cycle of low wages and low demand," warned a study from the Center for American Progress that ICCR gladly gave prominence to. "The simple fact of the matter is that when households do not have money, retailers do not have customers," the October 2014 report said. Companies were not oblivious to the bind they were in. As the center enumerated, two-thirds of the top 100 US retailers, in their federal financial filings, had cited flat or falling incomes among consumers as a risk to their business. Among them was Walmart.

Beyond all the private exchanges Walmart executives were having with ICCR and the others, the company also faced more public flogging. Just days after the release of the Center for American Progress report, OUR Walmart organized a protest outside the Manhattan home of Mr. Sam's daughter, Alice Walton. Hundreds picketed. "Walmart stole my American dream!" one of their signs read. Others called for a $15 minimum wage. "I can't afford anything," said LaRanda Jackson, who earned $8.75 an hour working as a salesclerk at a Walmart in Cincinnati. "Sometimes I can't afford soap, toothpaste, tissue. Sometimes I have to go without washing my clothes." Jackson was one of 26 protestors arrested for civil disobedience after they linked arms and sat down in the middle of Park Avenue, blocking traffic. Other protests were held that day in Washington and Phoenix. And the next month, on Black Friday, OUR Walmart stage-managed more than 1,500 demonstrations across the United States.

By this point, though, McMillon wasn't depending on anyone from the outside—not the objectors from OUR Walmart or any think tank experts, not an emissary from the White House or even Sister Barbara—to persuade him that he had to lift up the company's employees. During his own visits with workers, he'd heard more than enough from the inside. "The plan came from our store associates," McMillon said. "I'm asking repetitive questions all over the country: 'What do you need?' And all over the place they're giving me basically the same answers. Inventory was too high. Hours were too tight. And wages needed to go up." The wage piece, especially, hit home when McMillon was at a Walmart in Denver. As he and the store manager chatted about why it was so hard to hold on to good people, the manager pointed across the parking lot. "That burger joint pays more than I do," he told the CEO.

Bill Simon and his HR team had pinpointed what Walmart's employees wanted. "But it wasn't showing up in the stores yet," McMillon said. Once he and Greg Foran were in place, however, the effort became "much more ambitious," Gehrki said. They made it plain, she added, that "we don't need to tinker around the edges; we need a whole transformation" for Walmart's hourly workers.

Still, even then, a substantial package wouldn't just emerge—voila! It would require one more big nudge.

On February 6, 2015, Walmart's board of directors met in San Bruno, California. McMillon, Foran, Chief Financial Officer Charles Holley, and Susan Chambers, the chief human resources officer, were finally ready to recommend an increase in the company's minimum wage.

But even now—with all of the homework they'd done, with the great sense of urgency that they felt to rejuvenate store operations—McMillon and his team proceeded gingerly. "We were trying to balance everything," McMillon said, "including earnings growth and the pressures of that." Dan Bartlett would liken the calculus of attending to both workers' needs and Wall Street's expectations to "five-dimensional chess."

Their proposition: nobody at Walmart should be paid less than $8.25 an hour.

Getting there would move the needle some. Although only a tiny fraction of Walmart workers—about 6,000 of them—earned the national minimum wage of $7.25 an hour, there were many others who didn't make much more than that. The company's average starting pay was $7.65, about 8 percent less than what management had brought to the board.

The 14 directors went over the plan and, for a moment, it looked like $8.25 would be it. The discussion appeared to be wrapping up. "It was almost like it had already peaked," said Kristin Oliver, who was staffing the meeting. "It was quiet." But then Jim Cash, an emeritus professor at Harvard Business School who'd joined the board in 2006, spoke up. The company, he said, should go higher. "Jim was very passionate about it," said Linda Wolf, the former CEO of the global advertising agency Leo Burnett Worldwide and a Walmart director since 2005.

More than anyone on the board, perhaps, Cash knew just how much every dollar counted for many of those working at Walmart. He grew up in the 1950s in a segregated Black section of Fort Worth, Texas. His mom was a teacher. His dad was a mechanic for the railroad but always did something else, like fixing mufflers, so he could scratch out a living. "He'd come home from the night shift, get some sleep, then begin his second job," said Cash, who took on his own first job, in a hotel boiler room, when he was 11 years old. "Any time I started to feel like I was working too hard, I'd think about my father."

Cash, who was 6-foot-6, got a basketball scholarship to Texas Christian University, where he was a star player and became a math major—though he first had to get past the prejudice of his academic adviser. "His honest comment to me was, 'Are you sure you want to do this? You know you people aren't good in this discipline,'" Cash said. "My first instinct is I wanted to rip his arms off his body, but my high school coach, my parents, and everybody had prepared me for the fact that I was going to run into a lot of people who hadn't been exposed to African Americans before." Cash would eventually earn a PhD in management information systems from Purdue, before joining the faculty at Harvard Business School. In 1985, he became the first Black faculty member at HBS to receive tenure.

By the time a search firm contacted him about possibly being a director at Walmart, Cash was already serving on the boards of other large corporations, including General Electric and Microsoft. He was chary, however, about getting mixed up with Walmart, having read so many articles on how little the retailer seemed to care about its frontline workers (including, he would tell me pointedly, the *Los Angeles Times* series that I had edited). "I was really quite negative on the company," he said. Yet rather than just say no, Cash did what professors are disposed to do: research. Back in the Fort Worth area for a visit, he interviewed Walmart workers. A couple of them were relatives who Cash knew would "give me a really honest opinion of what their experiences were." Others were picked at random from three different Walmarts that Cash went into.

"The first thing that grabbed me was how different what I was hearing from these associates was from the impression that I had," Cash said. "And that really bothered me because I like to think I have a pretty high threshold for truth and that I don't get sucked into inappropriate perceptions easily. But I was so wrong, based on what I was hearing, that it really piqued my interest."

He wasn't the only one whose assumptions about Walmart had been upended. After joining the board, Cash met Dennis Archer, the former mayor of Detroit, who was a member of the workforce advisory panel that Lee Scott had assembled. As he and the others on the committee met alone with hourly employees around the country, the picture they painted didn't match what Archer was seeing in the media. "I would have thought if Walmart was this bad...we'd have people falling all over themselves: 'Let me tell you about this, let me tell you about that,'" he said. "That was not there at all. These were very proud Walmart employees."

The reality was, even back when Walmart was being spoken of in the same breath as Enron and the Triangle Shirtwaist Factory, there were still many workers who were grateful to the company for the opportunities it gave them. Trying to make sense of it all was a bit like parachuting into a big city and asking, "Is this a good place to live?" Well, what neighborhood are you in? Who are you talking to? With more than a million workers and constant turnover, Walmart was always going to be a corporate Rashomon.

As much as Cash came to admire the company, he was well aware that it was far from flawless. By 2015, there was no hiding quarter after quarter of sagging sales. But Cash, who was now the lead independent director, was hopeful that Walmart had hit bottom. "There is a scripture—Romans, chapter five, verses one through five—that you should celebrate in tribulations," he said. "So I am one of those people who thinks that when things are going really bad...I am being set up for something better in the future." That's how Cash now felt about Walmart. "As I saw these challenges develop," he said, "my experience told me that's when this company could really step up."

At Harvard, Cash was one of a group of scholars who had spent years analyzing what was called the "service-profit chain"—a set of relationships between profitability, customer loyalty, and employee satisfaction, retention, and productivity. Now, as he addressed his fellow board members, "it really did lay the foundation," Cash said. "And candidly, in my view, the starting piece was the context in which our associates work. A lot of companies call it 'engagement.' My label is 'belonging.' And belonging, to me, is what strongly drives the behaviors that I like to see in a service business because it's not just that I'm doing a job that I like; it's that I understand how I'm contributing to the success of this organization."

As he laid out his reasoning, Cash made clear that instilling this sense of belonging would be difficult, if not impossible, if Walmart's base wage was only $8.25. As some of Cash's university colleagues have written about the service-profit chain: "Putting employees first requires that managers," among many other things, "actually support higher wages." Staying away from rates of pay that were "dangerously close to minimum wages" was a precondition for reaching the ultimate prize: thoroughly delighted customers. "Show us an operating unit with higher employee satisfaction than another," the Harvard professors said, "and we can predict with a high degree of reliability that its customers will also be more satisfied."

Before he was done, Cash made note of one other thing. "There was an expense bucket that just jumped off the financial statements to me as being way out of balance," he said. "And I framed this in terms of we could pay for this wage increase just by doing a better job of managing that." The area he had identified was controlling inventory. This can be a big deal because, when levels get too high, stores are forced to sell goods for less than they'd like as they try to move merchandise. "You're just not selling through at full price," McMillon said.

But better-compensated employees are less likely to quit, and the longer they stay on, the more they learn to do their jobs well, including managing inventory. Shrinkage—losses from shoplifting but also from employees mishandling items or, less innocently, stealing things themselves—goes down. As one HR publication has stated: "Turnover and shrinkage are two effects of a common cause. Lack of fit and engagement on the part of employees leads to both turnover and theft in the workplace."

Cash had won the room. The $8.25 no longer seemed adequate. "Given everything that had been presented, it made more sense to do something more significant," Linda Wolf said. "Everybody thought more about it and came to the conclusion that it really was the right thing to do." Some were uneasy that Wall Street might come down hard on the company for racking up higher labor costs, at least in the short term. "But in the end," Wolf said, "it was like, okay, we can weather that."

Steve Reinemund, the former CEO of PepsiCo and dean of Wake Forest University's School of Business, was aligned with Cash from the start. In addition to Walmart's floundering sales performance, he was also conscious of how much of the nation—starting with the president—had homed in on low wages as a hot button. "You take the operational issues, the profitability issues, and the social noise, and you put it all together," said Reinemund, a Walmart director since 2010.

The three members of the Walton family who were on the board of directors—Rob Walton, the chairman; Jim Walton; and Greg Penner, Rob Walton's son-in-law—lined up in the same direction. McMillon recalled that before he got on the plane to go back to Bentonville, Rob Walton instructed him to "stretch yourself to see how much more we should do and how fast." They'd meet again, by telephone, a week later.

McMillon and his team were suddenly scrambling. "We didn't have that much time to figure out" the right number, he said. On the flight home, he told Oliver to re-run some scenarios greater than $8.25, which they had looked at earlier but hadn't fully evaluated. As the finance and operations staff did so, Greg Foran's directive was top of mind for everyone: whatever wage they settled on, it had to be justifiable as an investment in boosting sales, not just in making people feel good or shining up Walmart's public image. "This needed to yield better business results," said Lee Culpepper, who was vice president of corporate affairs. "That was the message." That weekend, Oliver and Melissa Kersey hopped in the car and raced to Joplin, Missouri, where the training pilot was ongoing, to see how that might be folded in.

As the final package was pulled together, some grew anxious. Kersey, for instance, had to pull her car over on the way to work because she felt sick to her stomach. She was stewing about possible unintended consequences, including how the stock market might react and how that could affect an employee whom she'd grown particularly fond of. The woman, who worked at the Supercenter right across from the Home Office, had been with Walmart long enough to have accumulated shares in the company, and if they lost too much of their value, she wouldn't be able to retire soon, as she was hoping. "I kept thinking about her and how tragic would that be because we're trying to do the right thing," Kersey said.

On February 13, the board met again on a conference call to seal everything. Six days later, the news was rolled out: Walmart would increase its minimum wage to $9 an hour by April and $10 by early 2016. It would also elevate the compensation range for each position within its stores, resulting in additional raises. All told, half a million workers would see their pay go up in 2015. They'd get a raise again the next year, along with more than half a million others.

It all felt momentous—and it was. Although Walmart periodically revised compensation in different locations to remain competitive in the retail market and comply with city and state minimum wage laws, it had never in its 53-year history implemented this kind of across-the-board increase. Doing so now, said Bartlett, was "strategically important—important for the business—but we also felt it was important from the standpoint of putting a stake in the ground and saying, 'This is a pivot for this company.'"

Newly hired employees would be brought in at $9 an hour and upon completion of the Pathways training program earn $10. This training, Walmart said, would also enable workers to "know what is expected of them in order to move from entry-level positions to jobs with more responsibility that pay $15" or higher. The company would also give frontline employees "more control over and ownership of their schedules," including the choice to "work the same hours each week and have a more predictable...paycheck." And, finally, Walmart said its foundation would donate $100 million over the next five years to support nonprofits helping retail workers advance their careers.

McMillon shared the news with his workforce by video, sitting at his desk wearing a dark sweater and a big smile. He would later call it "the best day of my career." Behind him on the wall was the print of *Convoy*, the totemic portrait of Walmart delivery trucks queued up after Hurricane Katrina. "We really wanted to demonstrate this year that we...appreciate the work that you do every day," he said. "Personally, I've been the beneficiary of a ladder of opportunity that was created within Walmart and have had more opportunities inside this company than I would have ever dreamed. And we want the same thing for you."

While he didn't serve up a full-on mea culpa, McMillon seemed to acknowledge that Walmart may have cut labor costs too much and neglected to invest in its workers for too long. "Sometimes, we don't get it all right," he said. "Sometimes we make policy changes or other decisions, and they don't result in what we thought they were going to. And when we don't get it right, we adjust. And it's clear to me that one of the highest priorities today must be an investment in you, our associates."

In the stores, emotions bubbled over, and McMillon's inbox was inundated with emails. One was from a store manager in North Carolina who had been with the company for 26 years. "I have never been more proud than I am today," she said. "I had no idea what you were announcing this morning. I gathered my team…and while we were waiting for you to come on, one of my assistant managers pulled up the announcement on his phone and passed it to me. As I was silently reading it, the tears started, and I could not stop. My associates noticed and asked what was wrong. All I could say was, 'You are all about to get very good news.'

"Everyone cheered and clapped, and there were more tears besides mine….They are very proud of their company, and I am too. We can now attract better, more qualified applicants. Our associates will take more ownership. Our customers will have a better shopping experience. And our sales will increase because our associates will have more buying power. Wow. Thank you, thank you."

Others were less gushing. "When compared to the $16 billion in profit that the company rakes in annually, Walmart's promise of $10 an hour—which even for a full-time worker is not enough to keep a family of four out of poverty—is meager," said Christine Owens, executive director of the National Employment Law Project. The *New York Times*, in an editorial, noted that pay for many workers would inch up by less than a dollar an hour. "A hugely profitable corporation like Walmart can readily afford to do better than those measly increases," it said. And members of OUR Walmart, who took credit for wrenching the raise out of the retailer, pledged to keep battling for more. "It pleased us, but they haven't pacified us," said Lisa

Pietro, a produce worker at a Walmart in Winter Haven, Florida. "This is just the beginning."

Yet, all in all, the response was favorable. Retail consultant Burt Flickinger III, who previously had given Walmart flak for its "complete breakdown…in staffing and training," now said the company was "going from being an unsatisfactory employer to a satisfactory one." At ICCR, Sister Barbara seemed gratified. "We have long challenged Walmart to show leadership on this score," she said. "While much remains to be done, we are encouraged by this positive step forward." ICCR's David Schilling held out hope that other employers in retail and fast food would now raise their wages too. "When it's a big player like Walmart," he said, "the ripples go forward." Sure enough, TJ Maxx, Marshalls, Target, and McDonald's would all soon follow with pay hikes of their own.

On a trip to Miami, President Obama called McMillon from Air Force One to salute him. "The president is going to continue to look for opportunities to shine a spotlight on those businesses that are doing the right thing," Josh Earnest, the White House press secretary, told reporters. Walmart, he said, "didn't make that decision to change their policies, give their workers a raise, give them access to more flexible scheduling procedures as a favor to the president. They did it because it's good business. It's good for their bottom line."

If only Wall Street had concurred.

When Walmart announced that it was increasing its workers' pay, investors were not enthused. The company's stock price fell about 3 percent for the day. As it turned out, however, those with misgivings about the added labor costs that the retailer was taking on only knew the half of it—or less than half of it.

In October, the Walmart executive team went to the New York Stock Exchange for their annual briefing with financial analysts. Back in February, the company had said that its pay raise for 2015 would cost about $1 billion in total. What hadn't been conveyed, somehow, was that the second year of the wage increase was going to cost Walmart another $1.5 billion. "Maybe we didn't give you enough information to do the math on the $10 jump," McMillon conceded during the question-and-answer session. The clarification hit the Street like a thunderbolt: for the first time, investors comprehended that, alongside other hefty expenditures Walmart was making in e-commerce, the higher wages would drag down the company's earnings by 6 to 12 percent the next year. Analysts had been forecasting a 4 percent rise in profits. It would take at least two years to see earnings pick back up.

"Retail history is very clear," McMillon told the analysts. "Those that are unwilling or unable to change go away; those that get ahead of the curve will thrive. That is why we are taking decisive steps now to change and grow our business.... When we stood before you a year ago our sense was that we hadn't been changing quickly enough or boldly enough. So we have been investing to get stronger and faster. Specifically, we are investing in people and technology to evolve our customer experience to serve them today and tomorrow."

Besides more pay and training, Walmart was also giving workers new tools to make their jobs easier. Employees were now using laptops and mobile devices to call up real-time information to help them serve customers more ably. Stores were being remodeled and thousands of department managers added. Numerous processes were redesigned so that just the right quantity of goods—not too many and not too few—were in stock and on shelves. Systems were streamlined. "Our objective is simple," Greg Foran told the audience. "Merchandise should only ever move one way in our business—from the back to the front and then out the door."

Foran tried to assure everyone that early returns on these investments were already being detected. In February, he said, only 16 percent of Walmart's 4,500-plus stores were meeting their internal metrics for providing clean, fast, and friendly service. Now, 67 percent were. "I want to be clear," Foran said. "We've still got lots of room to improve, and we have already put another line in the sand, and we have raised the bar higher for where we now expect them to get to."

But these "green shoots," as Foran called them, were primed to bloom. "As I get around the stores," he said, "I am seeing associates taking more ownership of their jobs....There's a sense of momentum starting to occur within the business, a changing attitude across those on the front lines serving our customers."

Walmart was mindful that shareholders were looking for more than soothing words. That day, the company also informed them that the board had authorized a $20 billion stock repurchase program. Some characterize buybacks as a signal that a corporation is confident in its future; others see them as a legal form of financial manipulation. Either way, Wall Street normally laps up such news in anticipation that it will goose the share price.

Not this time. As soon as Charles Holley, the chief financial officer, put up a slide showing the projected downturn in profits, investors began to clobber the stock—and they didn't stop. By noon, with the analysts' meeting still going, more than 30 million Walmart shares had exchanged hands, nearly quadruple its typical volume. Regulators were so alarmed by the freefall, they thought about suspending trading. As the closing bell sounded, the stock was off a full 10 percent, the largest single-day decline that Walmart had endured in 25 years. Twenty billion dollars in market value had gone poof just like that.

As disconcerting as it was to see the stock plunge, it made the Walmart team more resolved than ever to make good on their plans and prove the Street wrong. There was no turning back. "We burned the boats today," Foran said after the meeting to Jacqui Canney, who had joined Walmart in August as executive vice president for human resources.

As McMillon got in the car to leave for the airport, Bartlett was waiting for him, his cell phone glued to his ear. Jim Cramer, the clamorous host of *Mad Money*, the CNBC show for investors, was screaming at him. Walmart, he said, should have been more forthcoming about its earnings before the analysts' meeting. McMillon took the phone and tried to assuage Cramer, but it was no use. As he hung up, he told the driver to forget the airport; they were diverting to CNBC's studio in New Jersey so he could go on the air and try to explain himself.

"Walmart got taken to the woodshed today," Cramer told viewers. The retailer's earnings guidance was "so negative that even the announcement of a humungous $20 billion buyback couldn't give the stock any traction." After a little more of a prologue, Cramer invited McMillon to sit next to him and give "the other side of the story."

For the next nine minutes, with Cramer asking tough questions, McMillon gamely walked him through the whys and wherefores of what the company was doing, including the pay increase. "The real issue is," he said, "are we doing the right things to position Walmart for the future? Are we investing in the business to strengthen it?"

Cramer bought it. Those who've dumped the stock "don't really get what was going on here," he said five days after the first show. "McMillon wasn't so much cutting earnings as he was laying out a whole new strategy." It would take the market longer to get on board; the stock would continue to drift lower for weeks.

For any frontline Walmart employees who happened to be watching *Mad Money*, the brouhaha must have seemed bizarre. Tens of billions of dollars in stock value had evaporated, and mostly because wages had been raised to $10 an hour. "Ten dollars is pocket change," said Sanders Mosley, a Walmart worker in Los Angeles. When all was said and done, the average full-time hourly employee at the company was still going to be making less than $26,000 a year.

The uproar said a lot about Walmart. It said a lot about Wall Street. It said even more, however, about America.

CHAPTER 6

A Call for Justice

AMERICA HAS ALWAYS had jobs that pay so little, those who toil away in them can just about get by.

In 1845, the *New York Tribune* reported that there were about 50,000 women in the city—shoe binders, artificial flower assemblers, matchbox makers, and so forth—who were so desperate, they were willing "to snatch at the privilege of working on any terms." Working 15 to 18 hours a day, the paper said, "they cannot possibly earn more than from $1 to $3 a week, and this...will barely serve to furnish them the scantiest and poorest food." In the meantime, they had "absolutely nothing left for clothes, recreation, sickness, books, or intellectual improvement."

About one in four working-class families in Massachusetts in the 1870s had a difficult time meeting their basic needs.

"Their diets," historian John McClymer has found, "were lower in protein and higher in starch; they lived in 'poor' neighborhoods amid squalid surroundings. Perhaps as serious a deprivation as any, they were unable to afford those public badges of respectability—a 'Sunday Best' suit of clothes and furniture fit for entertaining." Around the same time, thousands of miles across the country, the pattern for those who pick our produce was established: big growers offered rock-bottom wages for some of the most backbreaking work imaginable. "The exploitation of farm labor in California," Carey McWilliams wrote in *Factories in the Field*, the nonfiction analog to John Steinbeck's *The Grapes of Wrath*, "is one of the ugliest chapters in the history of American industry."

Scott Nearing, an early 20th-century economist whose views were considered so radical that he lost his teaching position at the University of Pennsylvania's Wharton School of Business, determined that it cost at least $750 a year to maintain a "decent family standard of living" in an East Coast city in 1916. But 80 percent of adult men there were making less than that. "The chief cause of poverty is low wages," Nearing asserted. "People are poor because the rate of wages by the industries in the United States will not permit them to be anything but poor."

As America rapidly industrialized, one barometer of workers' distress was the ferocity of their response to their circumstances. The strike wave of 1877 began when the Baltimore & Ohio Railroad cut wages by 10 percent. John Lloyd, a history professor, has noted that "virtually every major urban industrial area from coast to coast was touched" during the unrest that followed, and in many places railroad men were joined by other workers who were experiencing their own "misery and privation." In 1919, some four million people—more than 20 percent of the US labor force—took part in work stoppages. Together, in solidarity, many sang:

> *It is we who plowed the prairies; built the cities*
> *where they trade;*
> *Dug the mines and built the workshops, endless*
> *miles of railroad laid;*
> *Now we stand outcast and starving midst the*
> *wonders we have made...*

The 1920s brought calm. Real wages jumped by about 40 percent between the start of World War I and 1929. Consumers purchased cars, radios, appliances, and other durable goods with abandon, while labor strife all but disappeared. "Coolidge prosperity" ruled the day.

Even then, however, not all workers fared well. In the coal mines and cotton mills, hundreds of thousands saw their wages erode. Racial and gender bias in the workplace was ubiquitous. And many workers, despite the gains in pay, were still not quite able to make it. Detroit-area Ford workers earned about $1,712 in 1929. Yet it now cost $1,720 a year for a family to live with even modest comforts in the Motor City. Given this, 44 percent of Ford workers who were surveyed said their expenses outstripped their income.

Income inequality also escalated during the 1920s. "Prosperity to the extent that we have it is unduly concentrated and has not equitably touched the lives of the farmer, the wage earner, and the individual businessman," said Al Smith, the Democratic Party's candidate for president in 1928.

Then came the Great Depression, and then World War II.

What happened next was the dawning of what many would come to refer to as the Golden Age of American Capitalism. Due to increased demand for less-educated, blue-collar workers and the government's wartime intervention in controlling wages, the gap in weekly pay between rich and poor got substantially smaller during the 1940s. The wage differential between the middle class and the poor also shrank during this time. Economic historians Claudia Goldin and Robert Margo have called this "The Great Compression."

By the 1950s, the compression stopped; wages didn't continue to equalize. But, in a break with history, they didn't become more unequal, either. An equilibrium set in. Those who had shared the sacrifice of war and depression were now also sharing the windfall of a surging economy. The biggest challenge "may be to prevent management from becoming overgenerous," the editors of *Fortune* went so far as to say. All boats, at least as measured along the broad economic spectrum, rose together through the '50s and '60s and into the '70s. "The United States at mid-century," Adlai Stevenson, the two-time Democratic nominee for president, declared, "stands on the threshold of abundance for all."

Unfortunately, that wasn't close to being true. Like the 1920s, the Golden Age wasn't golden for everyone. Women and people of color endured the most grievous pay discrimination (along with many other blatant expressions of bigotry). Through the '50s, "while white families were moving to the sprawling suburbs and savoring their economic prosperity," the social scientists Donna Franklin and Angela James have written, "Black families were experiencing economic adversity and increasing confinement to urban ghettos."

In his acclaimed 1967 book *Tally's Corner*, the anthropologist Elliot Liebow captured how Black men in inner-city Washington were resigned to work for wages that gave them no hope of ever getting ahead. "How much the job pays is a crucial question but seldom asked," Liebow wrote. "He knows how much it pays. Working as a stock clerk, a delivery boy, or even behind the counter of liquor stores, drug stores, and other retail businesses pays one dollar an hour. Some jobs, such as dishwasher, may dip as low as 80 cents an hour and others, such as elevator operator or work in a junkyard, may offer $1.15 or $1.25." Even at the high end, that came out to about $2,500 a year for a full-time worker—less than half the median earnings for men in the United States at the time. "The most important fact," Liebow said, "is that a man who is able and willing cannot earn enough money to support himself, his wife, and one or more children. A man's chances for working regularly are good only if he is willing to work for less than he can live on, and sometimes not even then."

It wasn't just Black Americans who were trapped in what Michael Harrington, in his 1962 classic *The Other America*, labeled "the economic underworld." "When the hotels, the restaurants, the hospitals, and the sweatshops are added up, one confronts a section of the economy that employs millions and millions of workers," Harrington wrote. "In Los Angeles, they might be Mexican Americans, in . . . West Virginia or Pennsylvania, white Anglo-Saxon Protestants. All of them are poor; regardless of race, creed, or color, all of them are victims."

In 1963, 20 percent of full-time employees earned less than $3,000 a year, which was under the poverty line for a family of four. The term "working poor" had entered the American vernacular. In certain industries, such as retail, earnings were notoriously low. "It is a fact that our economy has a lot of jobs that pay low wages," Labor Secretary George Shultz acknowledged in 1969.

And still, this was also undeniable: as US corporations flourished, so did a huge swath of the population. Compensation for production and nonsupervisory workers in the private sector, who make up about 80 percent of the American labor force, rose in lockstep with productivity from 1948 to 1979, with each climbing more than 100 percent during that span. "The deep nostalgia for that period felt by the World War II generation—the era of *Life* magazine and the bowling league—reflects something more than mere sentimentality," the journalist Timothy Noah has written. On the whole, "there probably was no better time to belong to America's middle class."

But then things unraveled. Pay flatlined, even as productivity continued to grow. From 1979 to 2020, the economy-wide income resulting from an average hour of work (that is, productivity) shot up by more than 60 percent. But average compensation—wages and benefits—for the typical worker increased by less than 18 percent over those four decades, according to the Economic Policy Institute. Put simply, Americans stopped being rewarded for their labor like they once were.

Analysts at the RAND Corporation have documented the same phenomenon. Their findings, published in 2020, show that a full-time worker whose taxable income is at the median—with half the population making more and half making less—now pulls in about $50,000 a year. Yet had the dividends of the nation's economic output been shared over the past 45 years as broadly as they had been from the end of World War II until the early 1970s, that worker would instead be making about $100,000.

Notably, it isn't just those in the middle who've been hit. The RAND study points out that full-time workers on the lower end of the US income distribution would be making $61,000 instead of $33,000 had everyone's earnings from 1975 to 2018 expanded roughly in line with gross domestic product, as they did during the 1950s and '60s.

Add it all up, RAND said, and the bottom 90 percent of workers would be bringing home an additional $2.5 trillion in total annual income if America's economic bounty was as equitably divided as it had been in the past. David Rolf, a longtime labor leader, has characterized the shortfall as "the two-and-a-half-trillion-dollar theft."

"From the standpoint of people who have worked hard and played by the rules and yet are participating far less in economic growth than Americans did a generation ago," Rolf said, "whether you call it 'reverse distribution' or 'theft,' it demands to be called something."

The RAND data also makes clear who the winners in all of this have been: the top 1 percent. If the economic pie had been divvied up since the mid-1970s like it was previously, yearly income for the average one-percenter would decrease from about $1.2 million to $549,000. The mounting fortunes of the 1 percent versus everyone else "explains almost everything," said Nick Hanauer, a well-heeled venture capitalist who is also a fierce critic of economic inequality and helped to back the

RAND report. "It explains why people are so pissed off. It explains why they are so economically precarious."

Somewhat counterintuitively, the proportion of low-paid workers in the United States has actually remained fairly constant over the past 50 years, hovering between 25 and 30 percent or so of the labor force. (This is when defining "low-paid" as many economists do: two-thirds of the median hourly wage for all full-time workers, which equals about $14 an hour today.) But to leave it at that is to miss much of the story. The American economy is much different than it was 50 years ago. Total output is more than 20 times larger than it was in 1970. Total household net worth is nearly 40 times larger. "There is so much more wealth now," said Michael Schultz, a scholar of low-paid work at NORC, a social research organization affiliated with the University of Chicago. "But instead of using that wealth to lift a lot of boats, we've just funneled it to the top."

Beyond pay, other aspects of job quality have deteriorated over the past 50 years, including company-provided health and retirement benefits and employment security. "The whole social contract has been ruptured," said Arne Kalleberg, a sociologist at the University of North Carolina at Chapel Hill who has done extensive research into good jobs and bad ones. This shift in risk and responsibility from corporate America onto the shoulders of individual workers has left many worse off, their bank accounts bare.

Incomes are also much more volatile than they were 50 years ago, saddling many with chronic anxiety—"a feeling of walking a tightrope with a fear that the next misstep or piece of bad luck could be the one that knocks a family off course, perhaps irretrievably," as Jonathan Morduch and Rachel Schneider have described it in *The Financial Diaries: How American Families Cope in a World of Uncertainty*.

While there is no single reason for the increasing prevalence of spikes and drops in the amount of money that people make, irregular work schedules are largely to blame. Over the past 15 years, more and more retailers and fast-food chains, among others, have used computer algorithms to track daily store traffic and assign shifts with the goal of ensuring that they have enough staff when consumer demand is high, but then eliminating "excess labor" when demand is projected to be slack. For companies, this continual recalibration presumably brings efficiency. For workers, such "just-in-time scheduling," with its undependable hours and income, undoubtedly brings pain.

Survey data collected between 2017 and 2019 from more than 37,000 frontline employees at 127 of the country's biggest retail and food-service companies showed that two-thirds receive less than two weeks' notice of their work schedules, and half get less than a week's notice. Last-minute changes are common, and it's not unusual for shifts to be canceled outright. Arranging childcare is extremely tough when trying to deal with such inconsistent schedules, and it's practically impossible to go to school or take a second job. It can also make it trickier for low-paid workers to be eligible for government safety-net programs. Unsurprisingly, researchers have found that those with the most unpredictable schedules and the least stable hours have particularly high incidences of hunger and strain the most to pay their bills.

The size of the US workforce has about doubled over the past 50 years, as well. This means that, in aggregate terms, there are now many more low-paid workers than there were in the early 1970s. In sheer numbers, America's pool of low-paid labor has become so massive—between 30 million and 50 million, depending on how you count it—that, as a society, we don't think too much about these people anymore. Their plight has become normalized, rationalized, shrugged off, swept aside. "When's the last time you sold something to pay a bill?" Emily Guendelsberger asks in her book *On the Clock*. "Have you gone to work sick because you can't afford to take unpaid time off? . . . Have you recently overdrawn your checking account, or had all your credit cards declined, or put exactly 10 bucks of gas in your car?" For those who can say no to such questions, it is easy to forget how many of the people around us don't have that luxury. We are like fish, failing to see the water that we're swimming in.

I'm not the first to suggest that we've become numb in this way. In 1959, Michael Harrington was reporting a piece for *Commentary* magazine about poverty in the United States when, as he recalled, one of his editors phoned him to say that someone "had just run across an analysis in *Fortune* that gave a much more optimistic picture." Why would *Fortune* be making things out to be so rosy, the editor inquired, when Harrington was claiming that "there were more than 50 million or more poor people in this land."

"I read the article," said Harrington. "*Fortune* was using the same basic research that I was quoting. The difference was in point of view. The *Fortune* writer focused on the development of the middle third in American society—the organized worker in well-paying industry, those who benefited from rising levels of education, and so on—and there was indeed a heartening rise in standard of living for these people. Yet, in the *Fortune* analysis, the bottom group was there. It was simply that these people were not commented upon."

Harrington's essay in *Commentary* became the basis for *The Other America*, which helped to spur President John F. Kennedy and then Lyndon Johnson to put together an ambitious antipoverty agenda. A. H. Raskin, a veteran labor reporter for the *New York Times*, said that Harrington's book was nothing less than "a scream of rage and a call to conscience."

In the end, it fell mostly on deaf ears. The government's War on Poverty "never truly mobilized the country, nor was it ever fought to victory," David Shipler concluded in his 2004 book, *The Working Poor: Invisible in America*. "Forty years later," he wrote, "after all our economic achievements, the gap between rich and poor has only widened.... Yet after all that has been written, discussed, and left unresolved, it is harder to surprise and shock and outrage."

We are 18 years further along now, and an ever-bigger army of low-paid workers serve us food and scrape our plates. They drive us around town. They pack boxes in giant warehouses and bring packages to our doorsteps. They clean our homes. They guard our offices by day and empty the trash there at night. They fit us with shoes at the mall and check us out at the market. They put up with us when we call to complain about something we've purchased. They care for our kids. They nurse us back to health when we're sick.

Yet most of us who are served, day in and day out, by these women and men don't register the depths of their anguish: that one in six can't come up with the money for their prescription drugs; that, even before COVID-19, about 30 percent of families with two working adults experienced material hardship, such as falling behind on the mortgage or the rent or their medical bills; that a third of those going to food banks are from a household with at least one member who has been working; that nearly half of Americans have only the slimmest of financial cushions and wouldn't be able to cover their expenses for more than two months if they lost their job; that homelessness is not just a manifestation of mental health issues and addiction but also of work that doesn't pay sufficiently, with more than half of those in shelters and more than 40 percent of those on the streets having had some formal employment in the year they were living under these conditions. "When it comes to poverty," Princeton sociologist Matthew Desmond has written, "a willingness to work is not the problem, and work itself is no longer the solution."

Our perspective has warped. When pay for most workers has stagnated for decades, $15 an hour sounds like a wage worth fighting for, even though it isn't enough for someone to afford the average fair market rent for a one-bedroom apartment in 29 states or the District of Columbia. Using the same criteria, it isn't enough for a two-bedroom place in any but two states, Arkansas and West Virginia.

Some employers get it. Bank of America raised its hourly minimum wage to $22 in 2022, and it will pay no less than $25 an hour by 2025. Costco—often thought of as the anti-Walmart—pays a minimum of $17 an hour, and more than half of its hourly employees make more than $25. Charter Communications, the cable operator, pays a minimum of $20 an hour. But these are rare exceptions.

"I was told growing up to go to college to get a good job," said Alexandra Parrish, a bank teller making about $25,000 a year in Missoula, Montana. "I followed that path. And now I feel a little bit lied to." Pearson, the education publishing company, posted an ad in 2021 for a part-time online writing tutor. The ideal applicant, it said, would have completed graduate-level coursework or have a degree in rhetoric, composition, literature, or English education; specialty coursework, a degree, or teaching experience in English as a Second Language; or teaching experience in developmental and first-year English courses. The anticipated starting wage: between $10.35 and $12 an hour.

A 2017 survey of thousands of frontline workers at Disneyland, which bills itself as "The Happiest Place on Earth," found that more than 10 percent of them had been homeless sometime in the preceding two years. Two-thirds couldn't afford to eat three meals a day. In 2020, employees at Blizzard Entertainment, the maker of *World of Warcraft* and other top-selling games, made it known that some testers and customer-service representatives were being paid minimum wage. One Blizzard worker talked about skipping meals to make rent and using the company's free coffee to dampen his appetite. Said a 23-year-old Starbucks worker in the Bay Area of California: "There definitely have been a few weeks where it's just like there's 40-something-dollars left, and I'm like, 'Okay, I have 11 more days to go on this, and I don't have much left in the fridge.'" Two-thirds of some 10,000 Kroger supermarket workers surveyed in 2021 said they weren't earning enough to cover their basic expenses each month, with 44 percent reporting that they couldn't pay their rent and 39 percent unable to afford groceries.

And on and on it goes. The average annual wage for the nation's 7.7 million retail sales employees, 6.2 million laborers and material movers, 4.1 million building and grounds workers, 3.4 million home health and personal care aides, 1.3 million public school teaching assistants, and 1.1 million security guards falls between $29,000 and $36,000. For the 11.2 million food preparers and servers in the United States, it's less than $30,000. Half don't make $13.65 an hour. And many don't even come close to that.

For tipped workers, such as waiters and waitresses, there is a federal subminimum wage, which hasn't been increased in more than 30 years. It sits at $2.13 an hour, with the stipulation that their set pay plus tips must get a worker to at least $7.25. But this presupposes that everything is done on the up-and-up. In reality, many bosses steal or withhold tips. Meanwhile, at some restaurants, "once taxes are taken out, workers still regularly get paychecks that just say $0.00," Saru Jayaraman, director of the Food Labor Research Center at the University of California at Berkeley, has observed.

For a moment, the pandemic seemed to shake us out of our numbness. The coronavirus prompted many to appreciate as never before the frontline workers who kept us fed and our family and friends from dying. We praised them and thanked them. We called them "essential."

"In a more humane system we would pay the people who do the essential work what those jobs are worth to society rather than treating them like just another cost in a business plan," the *Los Angeles Times* editorial board rhapsodized on Labor Day 2020. "But in this society we tend to reward celebrities, Wall Street risk-takers, and corporate CEOs with inordinate amounts of wealth that bear little if any relation to how hard it would be to get along without them. In this system, we don't signal the value of a job by how much we pay people to do it. Otherwise, the salary tables would have been turned generations ago."

The following month, the Brookings Institution reported that most large retailers had stopped issuing the special hazard pay—"hero pay," some had named it—that they had given to workers when COVID-19 first spread. The pullback had come, Brookings said, "despite many companies earning record sales, eye-popping profits, and soaring stock prices."

A year after that, in the fall of 2021, nearly six in 10 households with annual income of less than $50,000 said they'd faced "serious financial problems" over the previous few months. Three in 10 had chewed through all of their savings and had nothing left to fall back on, even as a new COVID variant was playing havoc with people's lives. Three rounds of stimulus checks and other funds flowing from Washington had provided relief—but only to a point. "While federal economic assistance has helped millions of families, short-term help is not enough to solve deeply entrenched inequities," said Richard Besser, president of the Robert Wood Johnson Foundation.

In their paper, the Brookings team gave voice to several essential workers. One was Lisa Harris, a cashier at a Kroger outside of Richmond, Virginia. Although she was making about $13.50 an hour, many others at the supermarket chain were bringing in only about $10. "I have coworkers that serve people every day," Harris said, "and then have to go pay for their own groceries with food stamps." She herself was more fortunate. "I am very lucky that my boyfriend works in pizza because that is our survival food," she said. "If we can't afford to buy food, he brings home a pizza."

Another of the workers in the study was Yvette Beatty, a 60-year-old home health aide in Philadelphia. Two of her children had lost their jobs during COVID, and Beatty was now trying to take care of her family of seven on $12.75 an hour. Sometimes, she had to choose between food and medicine. She stretched wherever she could.

"It's very hard," she said. "Thank God for noodles."

In a small room in the back of the Walmart in Lake Elsinore, I pulled out a chart from the Economic Policy Institute showing how productivity has gone up three and a half times faster than compensation for the vast majority of American workers since 1979—and how this has been a sharp deviation from the three decades after World War II, when the fruits of economic progress were more widely shared.

"So, I'm curious," I said to Doug McMillon, after walking him through the numbers and sliding the piece of paper in front of him. "What do you think happened?"

"What goes through my mind is the role of technology," McMillon said. "And I don't know how to solve this completely as a society, so I'll just think out loud with you." He paused for an instant, and then he talked about how a software company can generate economic value with far fewer people than, say, an automaker. As to his own industry, he said: "Should the world pay a cashier more every year to have that job track what's happening with productivity" on a national scale? "Or should the new jobs that are more forward-looking carry higher wage rates?" He wondered what might happen to that cashier if the pay floor moved up too high or too fast, implying that companies might then introduce so much automation, such jobs would be wiped out altogether. "How do you avoid some sort of unemployment crisis?" he asked.

McMillon leaned in and put his finger on the part of the graph indicating decades of flat wages. "When I look at that line, I don't like it," he said. "I would like to see this line go up more. But there should be some benefits from productivity driven by technology. And as a country, we should be investing in education . . . and other things such that we're creating the jobs of the future. And I'm concerned that we're not doing that."

Many economists would agree with him. A long-popular explanation for lagging wages is what is known as "skill-biased technological change." That's a fancy way of saying that all too many workers haven't acquired the skills necessary to keep up with what businesses most need to hire for, especially as computerization, robots, and artificial intelligence have recast the workplace, negating the need for humans to carry out routine tasks.

Michael Harrington saw signs of this even in the 1950s and '60s. "A generation ago in American life," he wrote, "the majority of the working people did not have high-school educations. But at that time, industry was organized on a lower level of skill and competence. And there was sort of a continuum in the shop: the youth who left school at 16 could begin as a laborer, and gradually pick up skill as he went along. Today the situation is quite different. The good jobs require much more academic preparation, much more skill from the very outset."

Sociologist William Julius Wilson identified the same trend as he teased apart what had caused a Black underclass to arise in urban centers across America in the 1970s and '80s. As manufacturing plants closed in cities and were replaced by businesses that revolved around the processing and exchange of information, Wilson wrote, it led to "a serious mismatch between the current education distribution of minority residents" and the types of good jobs available. More recently, in tracing the decline of the white working class—for whom the mortality rate has risen sharply over the past 20 years because of drugs, alcohol, and suicide—economists Anne Case and Angus Deaton have also cited skill-biased technological change, along with other factors. "The rewards to a life of work," they write in *Deaths of Despair and the Future of Capitalism*, "are turning against those without a bachelor's degree."

Other experts put the emphasis elsewhere. Some point to evidence that globalization, especially competition from China, has pushed US workers out of higher-paying manufacturing jobs. Some have keyed in on the concentration of power among a relatively small number of corporations, giving them the ability to hold down workers' wages. Some are worried about the "fissuring of work"—the growing use of contractors and temps rather than full employees. And some have called attention to the dwindling of organized labor, a 40-plus-year atrophying that has stemmed partly from unions' own mistakes but, above all, from businesses hellbent on doing whatever it takes, whether legal or illegal, to crush them. (Even in 2021, when power seemed to tilt in workers' favor and there was an upswing in the number of strikes, the private-sector unionization rate actually went down a couple of ticks to 6.1 percent.)

Based on my own reading of history, I believe that plenty of Americans have been beset by each of these things, though I put more weight on the busting of unions and the destabilizing of other institutions that once empowered and protected workers than I do on technology, globalization, or corporate concentration. I also believe that this confluence of forces has been supercharged by a change in corporate culture.

After World War II, the prevailing attitude among executives was what we now call "stakeholder capitalism." Back then, though, it was just capitalism. General Motors, for example, said in 1950 that it was "in business to make a profit" so it could "pay for research and improved tools and methods" in order to turn out better products for its customers; "provide jobs and opportunities for employees"; "earn a satisfactory return for investors"; "help others progress, including dealers and suppliers"; and "pay our share of the heavy cost of government." Many other large companies adopted a similarly well-rounded position.

But over time, this approach to running a corporation fell out of favor. A band of activist shareholders—"raiders," as they were then known—pushed back against the idea that the interests of all stakeholders should be balanced. Having latched on to the theories of the University of Chicago's Milton Friedman, the University of Rochester's Michael Jensen, and other academics, they contended that a company's singular focus should be on boosting shareholder value.

Investors had been emboldened, in part, by the sense that if any corporate stakeholder had been shortchanged during the 1970s and early '80s, it was the shareholder. The Dow Jones Industrial Average had reached 1,000 in 1972—and, buffeted by recession and mediocre corporate performance in the face of intensifying global competition, it wouldn't hit that mark again until 1982. "Shareholders deserved better," said Steven Pearlstein, a journalist and professor of public affairs. "And boy, did they get their revenge." Maximizing shareholder value was suddenly the dogma of business.

Of course, putting shareholders first has never been an all-or-nothing proposition. No company would be around very long if it totally neglected its customers and employees. Rather, it's a matter of priority. When there are trade-offs in business, as there inevitably are, the pursuit of profit and shareholder value almost always wins out—in many cases, by restraining wages or cutting labor costs in some other way. This has had the effect over the past four decades of redistributing income from workers to shareholders. (Some argue that workers *are* shareholders because more than half of US households have some investment in the stock market. But this is bunk. Most of this investment is indirect, through a 401(k) plan, and the balance in these accounts is low. The only real investors are those at the top, with more than 80 percent of the stock market's value held by the richest 10 percent of Americans. Most people rely on a paycheck, not a dividend check, to live.)

Despite many a CEO plumping for stakeholder capitalism over the past several years, shareholder primacy hangs on stubbornly. Not that we should expect anything else. Those who don't make maximizing shareholder value their No. 1 goal may well find themselves in Wall Street's bad graces—and soon out of a job. At the same time, more than 80 percent of CEO compensation these days comes in the form of equity, a key reason for the explosion in executive pay since the 1980s. When CEOs contemplate how much the company's shareholders should be rewarded, they don't have to look very far; to paraphrase Pogo, they are us. McMillon, for example, was paid $25.7 million in 2022—$19.2 million of that in stock awards.

As top executives have become exceedingly wealthy, the distance between them and their own workers has only grown. This, too, is a departure from the past. "If you were a CEO in the 1960s, you lived in one of the biggest houses in town, but you didn't live in a different world," said Leo Strine, the former chief justice of the Delaware Supreme Court, a locus of corporate law.

The Brookings Institution's Katie Bach and MIT's Zeynep Ton, who have counseled dozens of companies on improving job quality for frontline employees, have run into more than a few blinkered CEOs. "When we break down workers' basic living expenses...executives are often surprised that even workers making what executives think is a 'good wage,' like $15 an hour, fall short each month," they have written. "They're out of touch."

In 2019, JPMorgan Chase CEO Jamie Dimon appeared before the House Financial Services Committee, where Democrat Katie Porter asked him how a new teller at his bank could possibly afford to live in her hometown of Irvine, California, given the entry-level wage being offered: $16.50 an hour. After taxes, she'd be bringing in less than $30,000 a year.

Porter laid out for Dimon what this would be like for a single mom with a six-year-old daughter. The monthly math went like this: $1,600 for a one-bedroom apartment, $100 for utilities, $350 for a car payment on a 2008 minivan and gasoline in the tank, about $400 for food, and $450 for afterschool childcare. She included nothing for clothing or medical expenses or the occasional field trip. Even so, this working mom—a composite character based on several stories that her office had heard, Porter later said—would sink $567 in the red each month.

"I don't know that all your numbers are accurate," Dimon told the congresswoman. "That number is generally a starter job."

"She is a starting employee. She has a six-year-old child. This is her first job," Porter said.

"You can get those jobs out of high school, and she may have my job one day," Dimon replied.

"She may, but Mr. Dimon, she doesn't have the ability right now to spend your $31 million," Porter said, referring to Dimon's 2018 compensation package.

"I'm wholly sympathetic," the CEO said.

"She's short $567," Porter said. "What would you suggest she do?"

"I don't know," he said. "I'd have to think about that."

Some business leaders have tried to understand what their workers are up against. About eight years ago, when he ran the health insurer Aetna, Mark Bertolini and his executive team set out to learn more about the lives of their lowest-paid employees. When the data came back six months later, "I was embarrassed," Bertolini said. He had discovered that thousands of those working for him in customer service, claims administration, and billing were reliant on food stamps and Medicaid. "How could we let this happen?" Bertolini wondered. "Here we are, a major Fortune 50 company, with employees who are suffering every day to make ends meet." Aetna, which was later sold to CVS Health, increased its minimum wage to $16 an hour in April 2015, amounting to as much as a 33 percent raise for some.

In 2018, PayPal CEO Dan Schulman had the same kind of epiphany. The breakthrough came when the company set up a relief fund for workers who'd encountered a financial crisis but found that some had to use it to meet their day-to-day needs. The point was then hammered home when a group of PayPal employees were volunteering at a food bank in Arizona and became aware that some of the company's own workers were going there for sustenance. Even then, when Schulman commissioned a study to ascertain how many of his hourly employees were hard-pressed financially, he figured that few would be. "I was almost positive the response would be, 'No, we're not, because you're paying so well,'" Schulman said. After all, PayPal had pegged its wages to market rates, or even a bit above. And yet two-thirds of workers in the company's call centers and in other entry-level jobs—more than 10,000 people in all—reported that they were having a rough time paying their bills. "That was such a huge wake-up call for me," Schulman said.

PayPal subsequently lowered the cost of healthcare for its employees by about 60 percent, gave each worker stock in the company, and raised its pay so that everybody would have a living wage in their local market. The company has also taken it upon itself to make sure that every one of its workers has net disposable income of at least 20 percent. This is the amount left over after all of the essentials, like food and housing, are covered, giving someone the wherewithal to pay for a child's education, an emergency, or the occasional indulgence.

After it implemented these changes, PayPal surveyed its workers again. Employees were four times more engaged and three times less likely to leave the company. The increases have paid for themselves through reduced attrition.

I asked Katie Bach from Brookings why more businesses don't raise frontline worker pay, considering the return on investment that companies like PayPal have realized. She said she has heard all sorts of reasons from executives. Some don't have confidence that there will be a big enough return. Some are convinced, as Schulman originally was, that they already pay well enough because they've compared their wages to others in their markets. Some always seem to have higher priorities. Bach said she has been told more than once, "We know investing in our workers is important, but right now X is more important." Some fear that increasing wages will limit their flexibility—what if the business undergoes a downturn?—or that investors won't be supportive, as was the case with Walmart.

There are other impediments, as well, she said, including that those with the juice to get a CEO to act—namely, board members and large investors—don't usually insist that wages go up for those on the front lines. "This is the biggest reason that companies don't offer better jobs," Bach said. "There are many things executives feel constant pressure to do, such as beating earnings guidance, staying relevant, innovating. But no one influential is beating the drum for good jobs."

From what Bach has seen, prejudice is also at play. "Many executives equate low-wage with low-skill and low-value," she said. "A not-insignificant percentage believe their workers are lazy, unreliable, undisciplined, and maybe even criminal. This makes it hard for executives to believe that higher pay could be a good business decision." She added that this also diminishes "a sense of moral urgency, which might otherwise be a motivator."

This concept of "low-skill" jobs warranting lesser pay than "high-skill" jobs is part and parcel of the way that many of those with the most prestige—not just CEOs—look at the world. As journalist Annie Lowrey has put it, "any number of white papers, panels, and conference colloquiums will tell you" that the nation is full of people "without the credentials and chops to succeed in tomorrow's economy."

But these "elite policy conversations," as Lowrey has written, are "deeply problematic," if for no other reason than "the term *low-skill* as we use it is often derogatory, a socially sanctioned slur Davos types casually lob at millions of American workers, disproportionately Black and Latino, immigrant, and low-income." Classifying workers as low-skill makes them "the problem, rather than American labor standards, racism and sexism, and social and educational infrastructure. It is a cancerous little phrase, *low-skill*."

It is also very frequently inaccurate. A 2020 analysis of government data by the nonprofit Opportunity@Work and the consulting firm Accenture found that there are some 35 million workers, many of them low-paid, whose current job calls for many of the same skills that other jobs in their geographic area do—but those other jobs pay an average of 70 percent more. For instance, to be a good customer service representative (supposedly a "low-skill" position), you need to be an active learner and an active listener, be socially perceptive and persuasive, read well, and think critically. A capable human resources specialist must possess these very same abilities. Yet at the time of the study, customer service reps in Washington, DC, made $15.90 an hour; HR specialists earned $28.20.

"What are the jobs that we blithely assume anyone can do?" asked Byron Auguste, the former White House official who advised Walmart to raise its wages and now heads Opportunity@Work, which seeks to help more Americans achieve upward mobility in the labor market. "Restaurant servers juggle five or six tables at a time, preempting customers' needs and keeping a high-stakes, continuously recalibrating to-do list in their heads. Caregivers administer drugs and nurse our loved ones through what can be the most difficult times of their lives. Migrant workers acquire, deploy, and pass on a deep understanding" of crop patterns.

"Such jobs," Auguste said, "require optimizing time tradeoffs, quality control, emotional intelligence, and project management."

Or take the cashier that Doug McMillon invoked when he brought up the need to be careful about increasing pay too hastily. Over the past 30 years, retail industry productivity has more than doubled—and it's certainly logical to think that the skills mastered by cashiers and other frontline workers had something to do with that. Yet their real wages have barely moved during that timeframe.

All of which is to say, these are not low-skill jobs. They are just low-paid.

In late 2016, Doug McMillon went to Philadelphia to deliver the keynote speech at a conference put on by Net Impact, an organization of students and young business leaders who want to build a more just and sustainable world.

It was the perfect forum to take stock of how far Walmart had come as a socially responsible company—and where it was planning to go.

McMillon told the audience about how Walmart had responded to Hurricane Katrina, how those events had inspired Lee Scott to begin collaborating with the environmental community—and how this wouldn't stop now. In fact, McMillon promised that Walmart would meet a new series of sustainability goals, including becoming "the first retailer with approved science-based targets designed to achieve emissions reduction in our own operations and supply chain." This meant that the company would cut its discharge of greenhouse gases by 18 percent by 2025 and urge suppliers to reduce theirs by one billion metric tons by 2030. (Walmart would later pledge to achieve zero emissions in its own operations by 2040.)

Before he finished, McMillon spoke of Walmart's efforts to "provide our associates with both mobility and stability." He highlighted the wage increase that the company had just instituted and how it was going all in on skills training. And he put a face on these changes by relaying the stories of two hourly workers, Timothy and Kender, whose careers at Walmart were now taking off. "We started really focused on environmental issues," McMillon said. "But we understand how important things are related to people, and ultimately, that's what sustainability is all about, isn't it?

"We'd like to challenge other retailers, our own suppliers, other businesses in general, to join us in this type of business. We believe that it's our role, it's our responsibility. We believe that it's what our customers want us to do. It's what we believe the world wants us to do. We actually believe we're entering into a new era of trust and transparency. And when that light gets shined on Walmart, we want you to feel good about what you see."

To its credit, Walmart has steadily invested more in its frontline employees since that first pay raise in 2015.

Along with four other rounds of wage increases that took its average pay to $17.06 an hour by summer 2022, the company has altered the makeup of its workforce so that it's now composed of more than two-thirds full-timers and less than one-third part-timers. Six years ago, it was closer to 50-50—an upgrade that has not gone unnoticed by others in the industry. "I love when companies put their money where their mouths are," said Paula Rosenblum, managing partner at Retail Systems Research, a consultancy. "What Walmart is doing is very, very revolutionary. The entire store model for the past 100 years is built on payroll for a part-time, transient workforce so that the retailer doesn't have to pay fringe benefits or give raises. Walmart's decision to go more full-time flips this model on its head."

In 2018, after a campaign by United for Respect (the new name for OUR Walmart) and its allies, the company extended to its full-time hourly workers a benefit that had heretofore been reserved for salaried employees: paid parental leave—10 weeks for birth mothers and six weeks for other new parents. "For decades," said Katie Bethell, the founder of Paid Leave for the United States, an advocacy group, "Walmart has set the floor for worker wages and benefits in America, and today they lifted that floor." Within months, Starbucks, Lowe's, CVS, TJX, Dollar General, Chipotle, and Gap all followed Walmart's lead and strengthened their paid-leave programs (though, still, only about one in four American workers has access to any paid family leave).

Walmart has also continued to refine its scheduling system. Until 2016, frontline employees at the company had little visibility into what days and times they'd be working. "You had a lot of unpredictability," said Drew Holler, senior vice president. After that, Walmart started to give workers a look at their schedule three weeks ahead—although, week to week, they still might have to come in at different times. Now, because of new technology and the initiative launched in 2020 to reorganize workers into small teams, the company is close to giving everyone three months' advance notice of their schedule, with consistent days and hours guaranteed throughout that entire period. "Seven years ago, this is where we wanted to go," Holler said. "It was the ultimate dream." (Making the system more flexible, by allowing workers to swap shifts at the press of a few buttons, has proven more difficult to accomplish.)

Walmart has also enhanced its training, as well. In early 2016, the company replaced its Pathways program with a nationwide network of academies that teach frontline workers new skills in customer service, e-commerce, and other areas of the operation. Some 2.4 million people have completed different parts of the curriculum. Graduates wearing mortarboards are feted at elaborate ceremonies. "The caps and gowns, the symbolism, these are not trivial things," said Anthony Carnevale, director of the Georgetown University Center on Education and the Workforce. "They are trying to create this feeling among employees that 'we are the store.'" Starting in 2021, Walmart gave its workers a chance to earn a college diploma for free, building on a previous iteration of the offering that cost a dollar a day.

Medical coverage has also gotten better. For instance, there are now free telehealth visits for those needing to talk to a doctor, nurse, or therapist to help manage high blood pressure or deal with the flu or cope with depression or anxiety. For those with serious maladies, Walmart has expanded a highly vaunted program under which the company covers the full cost of travel and treatment at designated hospitals for employees seeking certain cancer evaluations, organ transplants, and surgeries.

Besides increasing pay and benefits, Walmart has revamped the flow of work at its stores and equipped frontline employees so that they can do their jobs more easily and effectively. One of the company's guiding lights has been Zeynep Ton, whose book *The Good Job Strategy* stressed the need for retailers to "design and manage their operations in a way that makes their employees more productive" and actually "reduces the costs of doing business"—even while paying people well and investing in them. As Ton illustrated through Costco, Trader Joe's, QuikTrip convenience stores, and the Spanish supermarket chain Mercadona, this sets off a virtuous circle of engaged workers who take such good care of customers that the business thrives, allowing for additional investments in those workers.

Published in 2014, before Walmart raised wages, Ton's book used the company as a foil—a paradigm of "the bad jobs strategy," if you will. "Walmart is both famous and infamous for its determination and ability to keep labor costs to a minimum," she wrote. Its "choice to operate this way forces the whole industry in the same direction." The conventional wisdom among many company executives, analysts, journalists, and others, Ton added, was that "improving jobs would mean either that Walmart would make less money or that customers would have to pay more. But they are wrong. The assumed trade-off between low prices and good jobs is a fallacy."

Today, with top Walmart executives having gobbled up *The Good Jobs Strategy* and having sought advice directly from Ton, you can spot the kinds of investments in hourly workers that she encourages springing to life across the company. For example, "Ask Sam," a voice-activated, digital personal assistant, aims to take friction out of the workday by helping employees locate merchandise and answer customers' questions. "The right tools," Holler said, "can be the difference between fast and frustrating." In 2021, Walmart gave more than 740,000 frontline workers a free Samsung smartphone embedded with Ask Sam, as well as other features that facilitate online scheduling, clocking in, and one-on-one communication.

More significantly, the small-team structure that Walmart has put in place gives hourly employees added decision-making authority and new opportunities for advancement. The company's expansion into fields such as healthcare is also creating new promotional ladders for people. In April 2022, Walmart said it was looking to train hundreds of its workers to become truck drivers for its private fleet—a job that pays up to $110,000 a year to start. In June, it raised wages for its pharmacy technicians. That Walmart workers might be better off if they "can go to another company... and make more money and develop," as Bill Simon remarked back in 2014, isn't something that any executive would express now. "We want people to be able to find a path to a great career," said John Furner, who in 2019 took over for Greg Foran as head of Walmart's US business.

Even before all of these latest improvements, Walmart's investments in its workforce had begun to pay off. By 2016, its customer satisfaction scores were going up. Sales were rising—and haven't stopped since. McMillon told me the company has had more job applicants, and higher-quality ones, since 2015. Turnover is down. If I had to pick between working in a frontline job at Walmart or Amazon, it wouldn't be close. Amazon, though it pays a bit more, is a far more ruthless place to work, with over-the-top monitoring of employee output that has led to high rates of injury. As they planned to pilot an internal company messaging app in spring 2022, Amazon executives discussed banning certain words and phrases from the platform, including "union," "pay raise," "injustice," and "living wage."

Nor is Walmart done. "We're making progress, and we have more progress to make," Furner said. He can foresee Walmart's minimum wage rising to $15 an hour. And a few years after that, he said, "it won't be $15. It'll be something more."

He wasn't the only Walmart executive to tell me something like this. "We're an inch into a mile-long journey," said Julie Murphy, the head of human resources for Walmart's US operations. Some may find this reassuring. To me, it is precisely where the trouble lies.

However much you think that Walmart has moved in terms of the way it treats its workers—an inch, a few feet, several yards, most of that mile—there is no trivializing what it took to get this far. Frontline workers, union leaders, nuns, newspaper reporters, politicians, executives, and board members all pushed, some of them for years and years.

And after all of that—after all the protests and HR focus groups, the headlines and hearings, the self-congratulatory speeches and board meetings—here's where Walmart landed: as of summer 2022, at least half of its US hourly workers still made less than $29,000 a year, many of them a fair bit less, given Walmart's starting wage of $12 an hour. (I say "at least" half because Walmart wouldn't tell me what its median wage in the United States is, so I based this instead on the average wage, which is reported. That calculation skews in the company's favor because at an employer like Walmart, the average is invariably higher than the median.) The less than $29,000 covers both full-time and part-time workers, including part-timers who prefer a limited schedule. But even if you use average hours for just the full-timers, their pay still comes in under $32,000 a year.

Twenty-nine thousand dollars. Think about that.

For the nearly 800,000 workers living on less than $29,000, it can't be easy. When you earn that little, even the least expensive health coverage that Walmart provides can quickly become out of reach, with a deductible devouring more than 5 percent of your annual income if you get sick. That's called being "underinsured." It follows, then, that in the six states that reported data in 2020, more than 10,000 Walmart workers were on Medicaid. More than 14,000 were on food stamps in the nine states that reported those figures.

Walmart howled when these numbers were disclosed. "If not for the employment access Walmart and other companies provide," a spokeswoman said, "many more people would be dependent on government assistance." That is indisputably correct, but it is still not unreasonable to ask why anybody working for a company with billions of dollars a year in profit should have a single worker on public aid.

"What does one do with a billion dollars when people are starving in this world?" asked JoAnne Bland, a civil rights activist in Alabama.

Bland and McMillon are not strangers. Several years ago, a group from Walmart, including the CEO, traveled to the South to learn more about Black history. People of color are overrepresented in low-paying jobs, and Walmart is the largest private employer of Black Americans in the country. McMillon has been taking executives on these tours for many years—long before the murder of George Floyd caused one corporation after the next to proclaim a commitment to diversity and inclusion.

Bland, who has had friends and relatives who've worked at Walmart, enjoyed her time with McMillon. Sitting with him in Montgomery, she found him to be all the things he is: curious, humble, caring, sincere. "He was very down-to-earth," she said. But after McMillon was gone, she couldn't reconcile the man she met with the pay his company offers. "They know people can't live off those wages," she said. "How much profit do you need?"

In 2017, Walmart began making available to its employees an app called Even, which helps them to budget and save, as well as access a portion of their wages ahead of payday. Hundreds of thousands of employees use Even. But are we to view this as a valuable perk, or as an admission by Walmart that many of its workers don't have enough money to make it to the next pay cycle? "It sounds like this may be a useful service," said Paul Sonn, general counsel of the National Employment Law

Project. "But it doesn't tackle the fundamental problem Walmart workers suffer. Their paychecks are too small."

Some continue to push for more. The Roosevelt Institute in 2018 released a study that estimated Walmart could give its frontline workers an enormous wage increase—more than $5 an hour—by diverting funds that it was going to use for share buybacks. From 2015 through 2021, Walmart invested $5 billion to $6 billion in higher pay, increased benefits, training, and education. Over the same period, it repurchased nearly $43 billion worth of its own shares.

United for Respect, which in 2015 split off from the United Food and Commercial Workers, is also still agitating. When frontline employees were given their new Samsungs, the group's director of corporate accountability, Bianca Agustin, chimed in: "Associates don't need free smartphones. They need a starting wage of $15" and a real voice at the company.

This isn't going to happen, not through United for Respect anyway. That's too bad. Keeping up a dialogue with the organization could be a big advantage for Walmart—a way for those in the "Bentonville bubble," as headquarters is known, to receive an early warning about a malicious manager in a far-off store or some other issue that should be dealt with immediately. For many Walmart workers, the worst part of the job is not the second-rate pay or benefits but "the sense of disrespect they feel from those who wield authority over them," Adam Reich and Peter Bearman, the Columbia University sociologists, have written.

Left unattended, these situations occasionally burst into public view, like when Beth McGrath, an hourly worker at a Walmart in Louisiana, used an open mic instead of the company's "open door" to air her grievances. "Attention Walmart shoppers and associates, my name is Beth from electronics," she said into the store's PA system in the fall of 2021. "I've been working at Walmart for almost five years, and I can say that everyone here is overworked and underpaid." McGrath accused her store manager of being a "pervert" and said she hoped that other supervisors "don't speak to your families the way you speak to us." She gave a shout-out to some of her coworkers—"Walmart doesn't deserve y'all"—and then she quit. "Fuck management," McGrath said. "And fuck this job." (Her parting words, which she posted on Facebook, went viral.)

Even after McMillon came in, however, Walmart has tried to muzzle United for Respect. In 2015, the company closed a handful of stores, ostensibly to fix broken plumbing. One was the Walmart in Pico Rivera, California—long a hub of worker activism. When that location reopened seven months later, nobody who had been at the center of the fight for higher wages was rehired. "The company under McMillon has continued to go after people who speak out for change," said United for Respect's Eddie Iny. In 2021, United for Respect recommended a "pandemic workforce advisory council," made up of hourly employees, to help ensure that critical safety and health information was reaching those at the top of the company in a timely way. The proposal was rejected out of hand.

The Interfaith Center on Corporate Responsibility, ICCR, has also stayed in Walmart's ear about paying its people more. For those with the temerity to question why Walmart doesn't do so, the answer you get is always the same—some version of "Our wages reflect the local market average for that type of job." Missing from this is any recognition that the market average has been weak for decades and that Walmart, as the largest employer in the country, has helped to set the standard. "It becomes a circular argument that Walmart is at the average," said Alison Omens, the chief strategy officer at JUST Capital, which measures and ranks companies on social and environmental impacts. "Functionally, they are the market." In 2022, JUST ranked Walmart very high for how it supports its communities and looks after the environment, and the company scored well on how it treats its customers. But it was near the bottom of the list for how it "invests in its employees."

Paul Polman, the former CEO of Unilever and an avid promoter of stakeholder capitalism, told me that he'd grade Walmart much the same. Like most big American companies, he said, the retailer continues to view its workers "more as a cost than as an asset"—its public pronouncements notwithstanding. "When you ask people what makes a company good, the dominant answer is taking care of employees and paying a living wage," Polman said. "All the other things you do don't make up for it."

This is not to make light of the steps that Walmart has taken. In the context of its own history, the company has evolved far more than many others. Its transformation has been real. But this is also real: if you work at Walmart, even after everything it has done to improve your job, there's more than a fair chance that you'll still be poor. Just because things are better doesn't mean they're good.

There are also people inside the company still pushing for more. But after a while, even the most well-intentioned recognize that Walmart will move only so far—and they need to come to peace with that. Danielle Goonan, who worked at the corporate foundation on training and economic mobility from

2016 to 2019, remembers one of her more idealistic colleagues conceding as much. “Walmart beats the bold out of you,” she told Goonan.

In 2016, as Walmart raised its starting wage to $10 an hour, *Fortune* named the company to its annual “Change the World” list.

“No issue is more central to this year’s contentious US presidential election than the anxiety of the average American worker about stagnating wages,” the magazine said. “But while Hillary Clinton and Donald Trump attempt to woo voters with their plans, Walmart is taking action.”

It is tempting to cling to the belief that companies like Walmart can change the world, especially at a time when government is so polarized and dysfunctional. “When the government is absent,” the PR firm Edelman has said, “people clearly expect business to step in and fill the void, and the high expectations of business to address and solve today’s challenges has never been more apparent.” Marc Benioff, the CEO of Salesforce, titled a section of his book *Trailblazer* to position the private sector as our savior: “Business Is the Greatest Platform for Change.”

I have always been a both/and guy, someone who has thought that both government and business have a vital role to play in making sure that American workers earn a decent living. But my last book was more in Benioff’s camp—premised on the idea that government was mainly there to set the guardrails and provide a safety net when someone really needed help; it was up to business to carve up the pie broadly and fairly, as it had after World War II. "Washington's prod can't alone turn things around," I wrote. "Corporate executives must step up.... It is their companies that must reinstitute a sturdier social contract with their workers."

My two-year dive into Walmart has caused me to reconsider. Yes, business can and should do more. Much more. But unless there is a government mandate, Walmart—and most every other company in America—will never move far enough or fast enough to provide people with a genuine living wage. Washington's prod is the only way to get there.

There is no mystery as to the policies we need to help workers regain their rightful share of the nation's prosperity. I'd start with these: rewriting labor law to expand collective bargaining, as well as to foster new avenues for employees' voices to be heard, including seats on corporate boards; making "full employment"—the point at which most everyone who wants a job can find one and a catalyst for rising wages—a primary goal of government; restoring overtime pay so that the majority of salaried workers qualify as they did in the 1970s, not just the 15 percent who do now; buttressing worker protections so that it's harder to pilfer people's wages or misclassify employees as contractors; and devising a health system that gives every American affordable access to good medical care, untethered to the workplace.

More than anything, though, we should require that companies pay their workers enough to live on. What this looks like is also not a mystery.

In the spring of 2018, as coordinator of a group called the Global Living Wage Coalition, Michelle Murray found herself in Belize, thousands of miles from her home in New York, urging a banana grower to raise his workers' pay.

"I get why I should pay a living wage," the farmer told Murray. "My question to you is, when my bananas are sold at the grocery store that's down the street from you, are those workers making a living wage?"

The answer was obvious; the average pay for a grocery clerk in New York is about $12 an hour. When Murray replied that they weren't compensated adequately, the grower seized the conversation: "Well, why aren't you doing anything in your own backyard?"

That question provoked a little shame—"I felt hypocritical," Murray told me—and a lot of thinking and planning over the next three and a half years. In November 2021, Murray unveiled a new organization, Living Wage for US.

The nonprofit has a program, For US, that helps companies around the country determine if they are providing a real living wage, shows them how they might remedy things if they're not, and certifies those that are. Dozens of businesses of varying sizes have signed on.

Rather than put out an assortment of living wages, which vary according to whether someone is single with no kids or a breadwinner in a household with dependents, For US uses one benchmark: what it takes to achieve "a decent standard of living" for a home with two children and two adults—one who works full time and the other who works about three-quarters time (a figure derived from rates for labor force participation and part-time employment). Included in its formula are the cost of housing, food, transportation, health insurance, out-of-pocket medical costs, taxes, retirement savings, childcare, other necessities, and a 5 percent margin for unexpected events.

Locking in on this four-person measure wasn't arbitrary. Consistent with widely accepted methodology used around the world, it is meant to ensure that a wage floor can support the typical working family—and, as such, it is a good reminder that it's mostly adults who occupy low-paid jobs in America, not teenagers.

Like other such frameworks, For US is place-sensitive. It fluctuates based on where people live and work among the more than 3,000 counties across the nation. For instance, the wage called for in Jackson County, Mississippi, is much lower than in, say, Marin County, California, outside San Francisco, where the cost of living is much higher.

But even when you account for these differences, here's what you find: 80 percent of Americans reside in a county where, to make a family living wage, they need to earn at least $20 an hour. More than 40 percent are in a place where they need to make $25.

The thought of requiring companies by law to pay $20 an hour may seem crazy when Congress can't get past $7.25. But what alternative do we have? Wages for low-paid workers rose appreciably in 2020 and 2021, even after adjusting for inflation, as a result of a tight labor market amid the pandemic. For instance, the 20th percentile wage earner (making more than 20 percent of the workforce but less than the other 80 percent) saw her pay rise by $1.05, or 8.1 percent, from $13.04 to $14.09 an hour over these two years. Yet this was a historical aberration; wages for this group rose by just 14.6 percent over the entire

1979 to 2019 period. To propel those making $14 an hour to a family living wage, this torrid pace would have to continue unabated for a full decade. For the 20 percent of workers who make less than that, it will take even longer. The market won't solve this.

As big a leap as it would take, a federal minimum of $20 an hour is where we need to get—and as swiftly as possible—if we want Americans who work hard to not merely eke out an existence. In some larger metropolitan areas, local officials should raise the lowest legal wage far higher than that. This rate should then be automatically adjusted upward as the median wage increases so that we don't have to relitigate a new living wage year in and year out. In the meantime, we should also expand antipoverty programs such as the Earned Income Tax Credit as a complement to a higher minimum wage.

It is sensible to pay teenagers, who are getting their first work experience, something less than adults. And phasing in a living wage, especially for smaller businesses so that they have more time to digest the cost, is appropriate. Ultimately, though, people's pay must reach what Republican Teddy Roosevelt said was "more than sufficient to cover the bare cost of living" and Democrat Franklin D. Roosevelt likewise said would be "more than a bare subsistence level."

To do anything less is unscrupulous. In his 2021 book *You're Paid What You're Worth: And Other Myths of the Modern Economy*, Washington University sociologist Jake Rosenfeld asks how workers at Burger King and McDonald's outlets in Denmark can make the equivalent of $20 an hour. For one thing, a sandwich there costs about a buck more than it does in the United States. "Profits are lower, too," Rosenfeld writes—but the business is still profitable. It boils down to "a different sense of equity," says Rosenfeld, an ethic that "paying workers too little to live on is morally wrong, and if that means some profit margin has to be sacrificed to raise workers' living standards, so be it."

At Walmart, executives talk a lot about how tight their profit margins already are. But Paul Polman, the former Unilever CEO, says that's a red herring. At a large retailer, he told me, return on invested capital or cash flow is usually "a better measure" to look at, adding that Walmart's free cash flow—the amount of money generated that is clear of all internal or external obligations—"is very healthy." Over the past five years, it has averaged more than $17.4 billion annually. *The Motley Fool*, which provides investment advice, has called Walmart a "cash cow." "Why do you think the Waltons are so wealthy?" Polman asked. "It's cash flow." Does that mean that Walmart can afford to pay its workers $20 an hour? In Polman's view, the answer is "overwhelmingly yes." "In a tight US job market," he said, "others will likely follow, attrition will go down and engagement up. It might be the best thing Walmart has ever done."

For a full-time worker, $20 an hour comes out to just under $42,000 a year—a rate of pay that is not lavish no matter where you live in the United States but that would allow for a little dignity. "It can't be paycheck to paycheck," Murray said. "Do we really want people not to be able to afford to eat properly?"

That the state should make this so is not a new notion. "A law requiring employers to pay a living wage" is perfectly in step with government's obligation "to safeguard individuals against violence and injustice," John Ryan, a priest and social reformer, wrote in 1906. "To compel a man to work for less than a living wage is as truly an act of injustice as to pick his pocket." More than a century later, David Autor and Elisabeth Reynolds of MIT's Task Force on the Work of the Future said it this way: "Countries have a choice about the level of economic inequality that they tolerate." As a society, we must ask ourselves, why have we left it to corporations like Walmart to make that choice on our behalf?

Twenty dollars is bound to come across as too radical to many, but we are without other options. As with climate change, we have put ourselves in a hole so deep, we will never get out of it if we think small. "The luxury of a leisurely approach to urgent solutions—the ease of gradualism—was forfeited by ignoring the issues for too long," as Martin Luther King Jr. once said. It is well past the time for those we elect to public office to force the matter.

If they don't, we already know what will happen: tens of millions around us will continue to struggle while Walmart, along with much of the rest of corporate America, is cloaked in the mantle of social responsibility.

ACKNOWLEDGMENTS

THIS WAS A fast book for me. It took just three years to research and write *Still Broke*—lightning speed compared with the five or more years required to conceive and birth each of the three titles that preceded it. Nonetheless, as always, the debts have piled up.

PublicAffairs has published all four of these books, and each time the team there has proven to be a writer's dream: thoughtful, supportive, prodding—but not too prodding. My editor, Ben Adams, pushed my thinking throughout the process. This was the second time I had the privilege of working with Ben, and I look forward to more.

Kris Dahl, my agent, has championed my work for 20 years now. I am lucky to have her in my corner.

Those at the Drucker Institute are more like family than colleagues. In ways big and small, they have my back—one of many reasons the institute is the perfect perch from which to write. I am grateful to them all.

As I puzzled out my conclusions, Miguel Padro of the Aspen Institute Business and Society Program was an invaluable sounding board. Gary Claxton of KFF, one of the nation's leading experts on employer-provided health coverage, shared his expertise. And Michael Schultz of NORC and Molly Kinder of the Brookings Institution made me wrestle harder with what it would take to institute a living wage in this country.

Writing is a solitary business, but my friends make it feel less lonely. Asking with genuine curiosity, "How's the book going?" means more than they can possibly know. A big shout-out to Jeff Strauss, Mindy Schultheis, Erica Huggins, John Huggins, Jeff Elmassian, Kristine Puich, Dean Parisot, Chesney Hill, Barry Greenberg, Kathryn Kranhold, Mark Arax, Fax Bahr, Mary Helen Berg, and Anne Reifenberg.

My children, Emma and Nathaniel, inspire me with their own creativity—Emma as a journalist, Nathaniel as a music artist. Emma also did me the favor of listening to much of the book read aloud, which helped me get the rhythm of the words just right.

Nobody has done more to nurture this book than my wife, Randye Hoder. She is the most perceptive reader I know and gave me valuable feedback on every chapter. It's only when she has signed off on a section of the book that I feel it is, in fact, good to go. More than anyone, Randye is also impacted by every book I write: the many, many hours when I am locked away, tuned out and unavailable. Still, she cheers me on, lovingly and with magnanimity.

Finally, there is my mother, Evelyn Wartzman. She passed away on February 6, 2020, at age 95 while I was in the midst of this project. My mom grew up in Baltimore. Her parents, both of them Eastern European immigrants, operated a tiny grocery store. They had six kids and very little money. My mom was unfailingly appreciative of the advantages that came her way later in life. She never lost sight of how people often struggle to make ends meet even though they are working their tails off. She treated everyone she met with genuine respect. I will forever be thankful for the way she believed in me and made me believe in myself and for the way she instilled in me the values that infuse my work. I miss her every day.

A NOTE ON SOURCING

THIS BOOK IS BASED, in large part, on more than 150 interviews that I conducted in 2019, 2020, and 2021.

But it also relies on the previous reporting, research, and keen observations published over many years by a large group of journalists, scholars, executives, and worker advocates. Without their insights, mine would not have been possible.

In Chapter 1, in telling the story of how Sam Walton built Walmart, Bob Ortega's book, *In Sam We Trust*, was indispensable. Walton's autobiography, *Made in America*, was equally invaluable. I also drew heavily on Nelson Lichtenstein's *The Retail Revolution* and *Wal-Mart: A History of Sam Walton's Retail Phenomenon* by Sandra S. Vance and Roy V. Scott. Also of great help was Charles Fishman's *The Wal-Mart Effect*.

In Chapter 2, while recounting the impact of Hurricane Katrina on Lee Scott and Walmart's early partnership with the environmental community, I largely retraced steps taken by Edward Humes in his book *Force of Nature*.

A Note on Sourcing

In Chapters 2, 3, and 4, scores of newspaper and magazine stories in the *New York Times*, *Washington Post*, *Huffington Post*, *The Nation*, and elsewhere allowed me to detail the battles between Walmart and various union-backed groups—and to feature the voices of frontline employees captured in those contemporaneous accounts.

Working for Respect by Columbia University sociologists Adam Reich and Peter Bearman was essential to understanding why it is overly simplistic to just label Walmart a "bad" employer; in the eyes of many of the company's own workers, it's not so black and white. Reich also generously provided me with access to their rich archive of worker oral histories, which I made good use of.

Bethany Moreton's *To Serve God and Wal-Mart*, Liza Featherstone's *Selling Women Short: The Landmark Battle for Workers' Rights at Wal-Mart*, and Annelise Orleck's *We Are All Fast-Food Workers Now* added crucial perspective.

In Chapters 4 and 5 and throughout the book, I leaned on the great reporting of the *Wall Street Journal*, *Los Angeles Times*, *Fortune*, *Forbes*, *Time*, CNBC, and many other news outlets to track Walmart's financial and operational ups and downs.

In Chapter 6, in exploring and explaining the history of low-paid work in America, I turned to a wide body of expert analysis. But none was more important than that of the Economic Policy Institute, the Brookings Institution, and the National Bureau of Economic Research.

All of this barely scratches the surface. If my narrative holds up, it's because of the strong foundation underneath it: hundreds and hundreds of articles from more than 80 different news organizations; more than 60 books; research from more than 20 think tanks and policy centers; a raft of corporate news releases, speeches, and financial filings; a trove of union material; court records and National Labor Relations Board decisions; government economic statistics; and more.

For a complete set of endnotes, please visit www.publicaffairsbooks.com/titles/rick-wartzman/still-broke/9781541757998/.

BIBLIOGRAPHY

The books listed are those used by the author, not necessarily the original editions, so that the page numbers cited in the endnotes will correspond.

Anker, Richard, and Martha Anker. *Living Wages Around the World: Manual for Measurement*. Northampton, MA: Edward Elgar, 2017.

Bergdahl, Michael. *The 10 Rules of Sam Walton: Success Secrets for Remarkable Results*. Hoboken, NJ: John Wiley & Sons, 2006.

Brandeis, Louis D. *Other People's Money and How the Bankers Use It*. New York: Frederick A. Stokes, 1914.

Brenner, Aaron, Benjamin Day, and Immanuel Ness, eds. *The Encyclopedia of Strikes in American History*. Armonk, NY: M. E. Sharpe, 2009.

Brinkley, Douglas. *The Great Deluge: Hurricane Katrina, New Orleans, and the Mississippi Gulf Coast*. New York: Harper Perennial, 2007.

———. *Wheels for the World: Henry Ford, His Company, and a Century of Progress, 1903–2003*. New York: Viking, 2003.

Bibliography

Case, Anne, and Angus Deaton. *Deaths of Despair and the Future of Capitalism*. Princeton, NJ: Princeton University Press, 2020.

Dauvergne, Peter, and Genevieve LeBaron. *Protest Inc.: The Corporatization of Activism*. Malden, MA: Polity Press, 2014.

Drucker, Peter F. *Concept of the Corporation*. New Brunswick, NJ: Transaction Publishers, 2008.

———. *The Ecological Vision: Reflections on the American Condition*. New Brunswick, NJ: Transaction Publishers, 1993.

———. *The Practice of Management*. New York: HarperCollins, 2006.

Ehrenreich, Barbara. *Nickel and Dimed: On (Not) Getting By in America*. New York: Metropolitan Books, 2001.

Featherstone, Liza. *Selling Women Short: The Landmark Battle for Workers' Rights at Wal-Mart*. New York: Basic Books, 2005.

Filene, Edward A. *Speaking of Change: A Selection of Speeches and Articles*. Madison, WI: Filene Research Institute, 2008.

Fisher, Andrew. *Big Hunger: The Unholy Alliance Between Corporate America and Anti-Hunger Groups*. Cambridge, MA: MIT Press, 2018.

Fishman, Charles. *The Wal-Mart Effect: How the World's Most Powerful Company Really Works—And How It's Transforming the American Economy*. New York: Penguin Press, 2006.

Franklin, Donna L., and Angela D. James. *Ensuring Inequality: The Structural Transformation of the African-American Family*. New York: Oxford University Press, 2015.

Galbraith, James K. *Created Unequal: The Crisis in American Pay*. Chicago: University of Chicago Press, 2000.

Gosselin, Peter. *High Wire: The Precarious Financial Lives of American Families*. New York: Basic Books, 2008.

Greenhouse, Steven. *The Big Squeeze: Tough Times for the American Worker*. New York: Anchor Books, 2008.

Guendelsberger, Emily. *On the Clock: What Low-Wage Work Did to Me and How It Drives America Insane*. New York: Little, Brown, 2019.

Hacker, Jacob S. *The Great Risk Shift: The Assault on American Jobs, Families, Health Care, and Retirement and How You Can Fight Back*. New York: Oxford University Press, 2006.

Harrington, Michael. *The Other America: Poverty in the United States*. New York: Penguin Books, 1981.

Hawken, Paul. *The Ecology of Commerce: A Declaration of Sustainability*. New York: HarperCollins, 2005.

Heskett, James L., W. Earl Sasser Jr., and Leonard A. Schlesinger. *The Service Profit Chain: How Leading Companies Link Profit and Growth to Loyalty, Satisfaction, and Value*. New York: Free Press, 1997.

Hollender, Jeffrey. *What Matters Most: How a Small Group of Pioneers Is Teaching Social Responsibility to Big Business, and Why Big Business Is Listening*. New York: Basic Books, 2005.

Humes, Edward. *Force of Nature: The Unlikely Story of Wal-Mart's Green Revolution*. New York: HarperCollins, 2011.

Jaffe, Sarah. *Necessary Trouble: Americans in Revolt*. New York: Nation Books, 2017.

Kalleberg, Arne L. *Good Jobs, Bad Jobs: The Rise of Polarized and Precarious Employment Systems in the United States, 1970s to 2000s*. New York: Russell Sage Foundation, 2011.

Kristof, Nicholas D., and Sheryl WuDunn. *Tightrope: Americans Reaching for Hope*. New York: Alfred A. Knopf, 2020.

Levinson, Marc. *The Great A&P and the Struggle for Small Business in America*. New York: Hill and Wang, 2011.

Lichtenstein, Nelson. *The Retail Revolution: How Wal-Mart Created a Brave New World of Business*. New York: Metropolitan Books, 2009.

———, ed. *Wal-Mart: The Face of Twenty-First-Century Capitalism*. New York: New Press, 2006.

Liebow, Elliot. *Tally's Corner: A Study of Negro Streetcorner Men*. Boston: Little, Brown, 1967.

McWilliams, Carey. *Factories in the Field: The Story of Migratory Farm Labor in California*. Boston: Little, Brown, 1939.

Miller, Douglas T., and Marion Nowak. *The Fifties: The Way We Really Were*. Garden City, NY: Doubleday, 1977.

Morduch, Jonathan, and Rachel Schneider. *The Financial Diaries: How American Families Cope in a World of Uncertainty*. Princeton, NJ: Princeton University Press, 2017.

Moreton, Bethany. *To Serve God and Wal-Mart: The Making of Christian Free Enterprise*. Cambridge, MA: Harvard University Press, 2010.

Nearing, Scott. *Poverty and Riches: A Study of the Industrial Regime*. Philadelphia: John C. Winston, 1916.

Noah, Timothy. *The Great Divergence: America's Growing Inequality Crisis and What We Can Do About It*. New York: Bloomsbury Press, 2012.

Orleck, Annelise. *"We Are All Fast-Food Workers Now": The Global Uprising Against Poverty Wages*. Boston: Beacon Press, 2018.

Ortega, Bob. *In Sam We Trust: The Untold Story of Sam Walton and How Wal-Mart Is Devouring America*. New York: Times Books, 1998.

Osterman, Paul, ed. *Creating Good Jobs: An Industry-Based Strategy*. Cambridge, MA: MIT Press, 2019.

Posner, Eric A. *How Antitrust Failed Workers*. New York: Oxford University Press, 2021.

Rathke, Wade. *Citizen Wealth: Winning the Campaign to Save Working Families*. San Francisco: Berrett-Koehler, 2009.

———. *Nuts & Bolts: The ACORN Fundamentals of Organizing*. New Orleans: Social Policy Press, 2018.

Reich, Adam, and Peter Bearman. *Working for Respect: Community and Conflict at Walmart*. New York: Columbia University Press, 2018.

Rolf, David. *The Fight for $15: The Right Wage for a Working America*. New York: New Press, 2016.

Rosenfeld, Jake. *You're Paid What You're Worth: And Other Myths of the Modern Economy*. Cambridge, MA: Belknap Press, 2021.

Ryan, John A. *A Living Wage*. New York: Macmillan, 1920.

Shipler, David K. *The Working Poor: Invisible in America*. New York: Alfred A. Knopf, 2004.

Stern, Andy. *Raising the Floor: How a Universal Basic Income Can Renew Our Economy and Rebuild the American Dream*. New York: PublicAffairs, 2016.

Stone, Brad. *The Everything Store: Jeff Bezos and the Age of Amazon*. New York: Little, Brown, 2013.

Ton, Zeynep. *The Good Jobs Strategy: How the Smartest Companies Invest in Employees to Lower Costs and Boost Profits*. Boston: New Harvest, 2014.

Troy, Leo, and Neil Sheflin. *Union Sourcebook: Membership, Finances, Structure, Directory*. West Orange, NJ: Industrial Relations Data and Information Services, 1985.

Vance, Sandra S., and Roy V. Scott. *Wal-Mart: A History of Sam Walton's Retail Phenomenon*. New York: Twayne Publishers, 1994.

Walton, Sam. *Made in America: My Story*. New York: Doubleday, 1992.

Wartzman, Rick. *The End of Loyalty: The Rise and Fall of Good Jobs in America*. New York: PublicAffairs, 2017.

Weil, David. *The Fissured Workplace: Why Work Became So Bad for So Many and What Can Be Done to Improve It*. Cambridge, MA: Harvard University Press, 2014.

Werbach, Adam. *Act Now, Apologize Later*. New York: HarperCollins, 1997.

Whitfield, Stephen J. *Scott Nearing: Apostle of American Radicalism*. New York: Columbia University Press, 1974.

Wilson, William Julius. *The Truly Disadvantaged: The Inner City, the Underclass, and Public Policy*. Chicago: University of Chicago Press, 1987.

Wu, Tim. *The Curse of Bigness: Antitrust in the New Gilded Age*. New York: Columbia Global Reports, 2018.

Zieger, Robert H. *American Workers, American Unions*. Baltimore: Johns Hopkins University Press, 1994.

INDEX

Index

Index

Index

Index

Index

CREDIT: JOHN HUGGINS

Rick Wartzman is head of the KH Moon Center for a Functioning Society at the Drucker Institute, a part of Claremont Graduate University. His commentary for *Fast Company* was recognized by the Society for Advancing Business Editing and Writing with its Best in Business award for 2018. He has also written for *Fortune*, *Time*, *Businessweek*, and many other publications. His books include *The End of Loyalty: The Rise and Fall of Good Jobs in America*, which was a finalist for the Los Angeles Times Book Prize in Current Interest and named one of the best books of 2017 by *strategy+business*; *Obscene in the Extreme: The Burning and Banning of John Steinbeck's The Grapes of Wrath*, which was a finalist for the Los Angeles Times Book Prize in History and a PEN USA Literary Award; and *The King of California: J.G. Boswell and the Making of a Secret American Empire* (with Mark Arax), which won a California Book Award and the William Saroyan International Prize for Writing.

PublicAffairs is a publishing house founded in 1997. It is a tribute to the standards, values, and flair of three persons who have served as mentors to countless reporters, writers, editors, and book people of all kinds, including me.

I. F. STONE, proprietor of *I. F. Stone's Weekly*, combined a commitment to the First Amendment with entrepreneurial zeal and reporting skill and became one of the great independent journalists in American history. At the age of eighty, Izzy published *The Trial of Socrates*, which was a national bestseller. He wrote the book after he taught himself ancient Greek.

BENJAMIN C. BRADLEE was for nearly thirty years the charismatic editorial leader of *The Washington Post*. It was Ben who gave the *Post* the range and courage to pursue such historic issues as Watergate. He supported his reporters with a tenacity that made them fearless and it is no accident that so many became authors of influential, best-selling books.

ROBERT L. BERNSTEIN, the chief executive of Random House for more than a quarter century, guided one of the nation's premier publishing houses. Bob was personally responsible for many books of political dissent and argument that challenged tyranny around the globe. He is also the founder and longtime chair of Human Rights Watch, one of the most respected human rights organizations in the world.

• • •

For fifty years, the banner of Public Affairs Press was carried by its owner Morris B. Schnapper, who published Gandhi, Nasser, Toynbee, Truman, and about 1,500 other authors. In 1983, Schnapper was described by *The Washington Post* as "a redoubtable gadfly." His legacy will endure in the books to come.

Peter Osnos, *Founder*